Green Roads in the

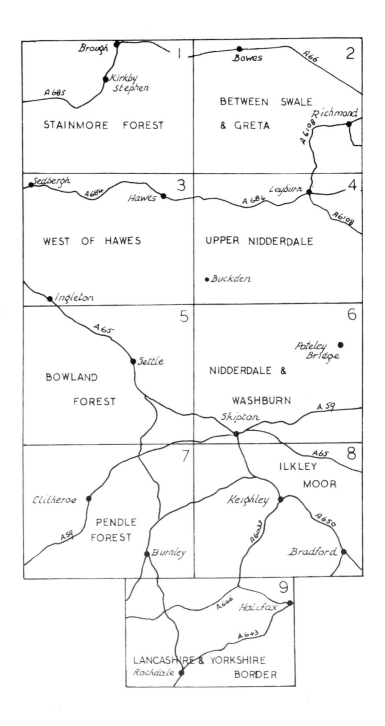

Green Roads in the Mid-Pennines

Arthur Raistrick

MOORLAND PUBLISHING COMPANY

ISBN 0 86190 184 3

Printed in the UK by
The Cromwell Press Ltd
Broughton Gifford, Wiltshire

For the Publishers:
Moorland Publishing Co Ltd
Moor Farm Road, Ashbourne, Derbyshire, DE6 1HD

Contents

Illustrations

Introduction

THE countryside is a true palimpsest to be read and enjoyed by those who care to take the trouble to disentangle the superposed scripts. The Ordnance Survey maps represent in strong red lines the newest script—the modern classified roads with their numbers, their straightened corners and smoothed gradients, overlying many older and partly forgotten road systems. The foot passenger who is wise, with time to spend and a holiday to enjoy, avoids the obvious pattern and looks beneath its harsh lines for something softer and older: the tracks that cling to the hillsides and the fell edges, that run unfenced across the moors, and that offer many a wild prospect of hill and dale that is seldom to be had along the newer roads. There are many roads and tracks of different ages, each with its own character, and each full of enjoyment for the explorer.

All dalesmen worthy of the name must at some time or other have walked with joy and gratitude along one or other such tracks and, perhaps, in his heart he poured blessings on the unknown makers of such a lovable way. The way over Horsehead into Littondale; parts of the road from Settle to Malham and forward to Kilnsey; tracks from Arkengarthdale to Bowes, and similar ways between every dale and its neighbours, are known to all who frequent the fells and moors.

A winter evening spent with adequate maps will soon reveal that these many fragments of green roads and bridle paths can be linked up into a few continuous ways, winding and twisting up hill and down dale, full of corners and divergences to ford a stream or to avoid a crag, but nonetheless on the long view, keeping a remarkably straight line for a score of miles, often crossing the whole dales area. They are sometimes traceable even further afield, suggesting that at some time in their history they have been highways of importance used by traffic to and from far places, a traffic now lost and forgotten, or shifted into the valley bottoms and on to new roads and railways. Pack-horse roads and bridges, drove roads, " streets " and " gates" are memories of a time when the byways and hamlets of to-day had a different importance and were vital parts of the economic life of the country.

Some tracks start out from valley villages, climbing steeply up the fell side only to die out on the peaty, high ground. Many of these are peat roads connecting the village with its moorland peat allotment and its hill pastures. Others connect the various villages with old lead mines or coal pits, mine roads which link the mines to one another and to green roads by which the coal was carried to limekilns and even further afield, sometimes seeming to come to a dead end and leave one stranded on the fell side.

From prehistoric and Roman times we inherit two " patterns " of tracks. The pre-Roman paths were almost certainly absorbed into and preserved as the upland tracks along the fell edges, often passing hut settlements and prehistoric sites of the Iron Age, like beads on a string. These oldest paths rarely cross a watershed and only descend to the valleys where the floor is rocky or gravel spreads keep it free from swamp.

The Roman roads are much more direct in their bold lines, cutting across the country and using the valley sides and gaps only so far as they can be fitted into a long distance plan. The great road from Bainbridge over Cam Fell, the road over Blackstone Edge, and the one on the moors between Skipton, Addingham and Blubberhouses and beyond are sufficient examples of this pattern, overlain on the country with the minimum reference to local needs and population.

The pack-horse ways, many of which provide our pleasant green roads, differ from these earlier patterns in their direct relation to the early economic and social life of the area they traverse, and in their intimate relation with the village pattern of the Dales. Pack-horses and ponies were the prime form of transport for approximately five centuries; largely developed in monastic times they were only finally ousted from their important position by the transport revolution of the early nineteenth century.

The monasteries spread their economy over wide areas. Fountains Abbey held by grant and lease over a million acres of land in Craven and from them drew great stocks of wool and other supplies. Bolton Priory had lands in Wharfedale and around Malham, Furness in Winterburn and around Ribblehead, Sawley Abbey in a large part of Bowland and around Gargrave. These areas again were heavily committed to sheep rearing and the production of wool, though in the case of Sawley a moderate amount of corn was grown on the lower lands of Airedale. In the case of Fountains and Bolton, sheep were brought down from the fells to Kilnsey and Malham for shearing and lambing, or were driven by easy stages to the Lake District for summer pasture on the estates around Watendlath and Keswick. The wool from the granges was carried to the Abbeys and to the river Ouse for shipment abroad.

Besides the wool, hides, coal, iron, lead, charcoal and peat were carried from Craven and at some seasons fish came from Malham Tarn. Corn and supplies of many kinds were carried back from east to west along these tracks. Crossing through unenclosed country the tracks took the shortest practicable route and in the course of much rough usage, were gradually cut into the hill shoulders as sunk ways soon made deeper by the weather. In soft country and on many hill shoulders, the tracks were paved with big stones, and long stretches of these are to-day the best preserved parts of them.

After the dissolution of the monasteries the pack-horse roads remained in use as the main ways of commerce. The small bridges and fords were the only important river crossings until the Turnpike Trusts found it necessary to enlarge the bridges or to plan new ones. A pack-horse train was made up of from 20 to 40 horses or ponies, with a driver and one or two attendants. The ponies commonly used in the North were imported from Germany where they were known as Jaegar (hunter) ponies, hence our dales form of the word which survives in place names like Jagger Lane, Jagger Hill, or in the surname Jagger, often given to pack train driver and attendants.

Each pony carried a pair of panniers or a wooden pack saddle, or perhaps a wooden frame called a crutch, on which two sacks could rest. The normal load was about two and a quarter hundredweights, and loads are generally measured in units or multiples of this. For bulky but fairly light stuff like charcoal, large square baskets called " bannisters " were used, and basket and bannister makers were an essential group of craftsmen for a long period.

The leading pony in a pack train had a harness of bells whose music marked the leader and kept the following ponies together. In some of the narrower ways they would give warning if two trains were likely to meet, so that a passing place could be chosen. The children of Yorkshire still, in my boyhood, played at " bell horses," many children in tandem with a driver, and the first child the " bell horse." The roads and tracks of pony trains can still be recognised over much of the remoter part of the Dales, where there was considerable traffic by the wool broggers, the collectors and givers out of wool for home spinning, the coal carriers, and others.

In addition to the local economy of the dales, two great traffics linked up the pack horse roads with a road system stretching far beyond the Pennines—those of sheep and cattle, and of salt. The cattle, sheep and horse fairs have disappeared, or are only a small relic of their former importance, and newer roads and motorised transport is now used everywhere. The Malham sheep fair in October, dating most probably from monastic times, developed in the eighteenth century into a great cattle fair lasting several weeks and visited by drovers from Scotland.

The drovers with herds of hundreds of head of cattle, spent many weeks on their journey travelling by green roads and avoiding the busier roads, coming over the Cheviots and along the fell edges where it was easy to get roadside pasture and rest for their stock. Along these drove ways there are many roadside inns and rest houses, many now in ruins, once lively centres of activity when the drovers gathered on the way to a fair.

Salt was a prime necessity for the preserving of meat over the winter, until the introduction of winter feeding for cattle enabled stock to be carried over from one year to the next. Prior to that time, most stock not needed for breeding was slaughtered and salted down in early November, and for that many stones of salt were wanted at each house. This was brought from salt-pans on the coast or from the Cheshire and South Lancashire salt areas, carried by pack-ponies along recognised " salt ways." These radiate out from South Lancashire across the Pennines, intersecting and linking with many more local ways. Salt way place names are abundant—Salterforth, Salter Hebble, mark fords on such a way. Salters Gate, Salter Lane, Salter Rake, etc. are all markers of these ancient ways, many of the names lying on what are now green roads or almost forgotten tracks.

There is no easy history of all the great variety of ancient tracks which have been made at all times through a long range of centuries for purposes now partly forgotten. Most of the upland roads were abandoned when the Turnpike roads were made for the accommodation of wheeled traffic, when gradients were chosen that were gentle and suitable for carriage and coach, and when towns and markets were of more importance than upland mines and villages. While it is not possible in a short space to give anything like a satisfactory history of the roads that are so abundant on the Pennines, something might be done towards drawing together a few readings of the palimpsest, sufficient to stir the interest of the reader and send him out to explore the great wealth of tracks which are still to be found and enjoyed.

It has not been possible, nor would it be desirable, in both text and maps to limit these strictly to what can be seen and properly described at this day as 'green tracks'. Year by year the pressure of motor traffic is securing the 'improvement' of a part of some of these tracks into roads which can be used by the motor car. Most long distance tracks are now broken up by long lengths of modern roads, being in their origin the shortest and best ways between market towns or fairs. Sad fragments of the old ways can sometimes be seen at the side of the modern road. The famous Mastiles Lane between Kilnsey and Malham is still a grass-grown road, the delight of hundreds of walkers, but the pressure for this road to be upgraded and made available for the motorist is as great as ever and shows no sign of relenting. Of all the length of the road from Fountains Abbey to its properties in the Lake District this is the longest fragment still remaining to us in something like its original condition and it preservation as part of our historic heritage is essential. Nonetheless it will have to be battled for.

On the maps many green roads are shown as they were in the time before the motor traffic and the Turnpike Trusts and the reader who is expecting a green road all the way shown will be disappointed. As the years go by he will become progressively more so unless we recognise before it is too late, that many of these tracks are a part of our historic heritage, many of them older and of more general public use than many of our cherished buildings, and strong efforts should be made to know them, use them and save the best of them.

1 Through Stainmore Forest

FOR a first essay, an area little altered during the past few
centuries will give the simplest picture, and such an area
is to be found in the wild stretch of country that fills the approximate rectangle between Reeth and Bowes on the east, and Brough
and Kirkby Stephen on the west. Taking the river Swale as
the southern boundary and the Roman road across Stainmore as
the northern, we have in this area a fine sample of the true Pennine uplands, mountain, fell and dale all well represented, with
a sufficient number of tracks to illustrate many different kinds.

A great part of this area belongs to the old Forest of
Stainmore, from which the New Forest of Arkengarthdale was
broken out soon after the Conquest. Near the centre of the
area is the well known and much publicised Tan Hill Inn, and
from that centre there radiates a fine plexus of very ancient
roads, many of them still " green roads " in the old, partly
grass-grown, partly macadamised sense.

Tan Hill lies between two types of country. To the north
of it is the broad Stainmore Pass, during the Ice Age the main
line of ice movement from the crowded ice fields of the Vale of
Eden and the eastern part of the Lake District. It is smoothed,
with all its irregularities and rock outcrops softened by a
thick blanketing of boulder clay. The clay surface supports
benty grass and heather, with soft swampy moors and streams
deeply trenched in their clay-sided gills. To the south of Tan
Hill, the tributary streams of the Swale cut deep into the fells,
through country with thinner glacial deposits, the rocks show-
ing as more frequent scars, and in the stream courses making
a great number of water falls.

The surface of Stainmore is mainly cut in the boulder clay
overlaying Millstone Grit, shales and grits alternating, while
the valleys of Swaledale are mainly in the Yoredale rocks, with
limestones, shales sandstones, with terraced hillsides and
stepped stream beds. Near the base of the Millstone Grit
series, around Tan Hill, there is the famous Tan Hill Coal, at
its best a seam of about four feet thickness, with another
poorer seam not far below it. This coal has been worked

since the thirteenth century, and has given a life to Tan Hill that it might otherwise have lacked.

Many of the roads that meet there have been used for centuries for the carriage of the Tan Hill coal to all parts of the neighbouring dales, and they owe something of their persistence to that use. Further south in Swaledale and its northern tributaries, the Yoredale rocks are traversed by the numerous mineral veins of the rich Swaledale lead mining field, and this belt on the north side of the Swale is crossed by innumerable green tracks running between the mines and the villages, and from mines to smelt mills.

The first road through Tan Hill that we will consider is the one coming from the north east, from Barnard Castle and Bowes. From Barnard Castle to Bowes the road has been modernised, but at Bowes we cross the river Greta to Gilmonby, turning along the road to the south-west quarter of a mile beyond the village. In a mile and a half this becomes unfenced road, skirting Gilmonby Moor, swinging round into the valley of Sleightholme Beck and going forward to Sleightholme.

At Sleightholme this track crosses another, one of the famous " drove roads " by which in the eighteenth century Highland cattle were brought from Scotland to the Yorkshire markets to be bought for fattening on the hill pastures of Craven and West Yorkshire. The track comes by Riccarton in the Border country, by Gilsland, and then by the valley of the South Tyne, over Yad Moss into the upper Teesdale. It crosses Maize Beck at the Birkdale fords and comes east to Holwick, then south east across Lune Moor to Grassholme on the Lune. Across the head of the reservoir on the river Balder by Blackton, it crosses Cotherstone Moor to cross the Roman road at Pasture End; it fords the Greta at Gods Bridge and turns into Sleightholmedale. It takes the east side of the beck to Sleightholme then keeping to the east side and well above the Arkle Beck it gets to Eskeleth, and there crosses to the west side, going on by the low col between Reeth High Moor and Reeth Low Moor to Feetham, across the Swale and so to Askrigg. From Wensleydale there are several branches of this drove road, one across to the great cattle fairs of Malham Moor, and others to Skipton and Otley.

Near the farm and on the south side of the road there is an interesting glacial feature. A small beck joins Sleightholme Beck, and as this beck is followed towards its head, due south, its valley gets larger, and soon opens out in the head of Mud Beck, a tributary of Arkle Beck, which flows down Arkengarthdale to the Swale at Reeth.

This deep channel at the head of Mud Beck is a glacial " overflow " at a place where the water which was impounded along the edge of the Stainmore glacier, towards the end of the Ice Age, found an escape across the watershed, gradually cutting itself this channel which was later abandoned and left as a dry valley. When this channel was operating much of the drainage of the western part of Stainmore Forest would thus find its way into the Swale, and not as at present to the Greta.

West of Mud Beck the road climbs the spur between Arkle Beck and Sleightholme Beck, to the hill called Cocker. From Cocker the road skirts the upper waters of the many small becks on the north slopes of Mirk Fell, but from Cocker to Tan Hill has been used in the new road up Arkengarthdale via Tan Hill to Brough. Kings Pit Colliery, one of the Tan Hill group, lies just to the south of the road in the head of the last stream crossed before the Tan Hill Inn is reached. The true continuation of this road takes south from Tan Hill, then goes due south-west, crossing the upper West Stonesdale Beck and continuing directly to Roberts Seat, crossing the southern spur of this at 1,759 feet OD.

There is the ruin of Roberts Seat House at the highest point, a former gamekeeper's house, long since abandoned. From Roberts Seat the road drops quickly to the hamlet of Raven Seat in Whitsundale. This part of the road is now only a green track over the open moor, but has been traversed by sledges and carts in quite recent years, although its older and more numerous traffic was that of the pack horse train.

For a short way the road now follows down Whitsundale past Black Haw and by Harkers House, then swings round the contour into Birkdale by Hill Top, just east of Birkdale Tarn. Below this house it joins the Birkdale road from Keld, and goes right up the dale to Lambs Moss, where the county boundary crosses the valley. At the boundary there is an old cross, called Hollow Mill Cross. From Raven Seat there is a less defined but more direct track, now only a footpath, which continues the line of the track from Roberts Seat House to Raven Seat, going up Ney Gill and joining the Birkdale road midway between Crook Seal and Beck Meetings.

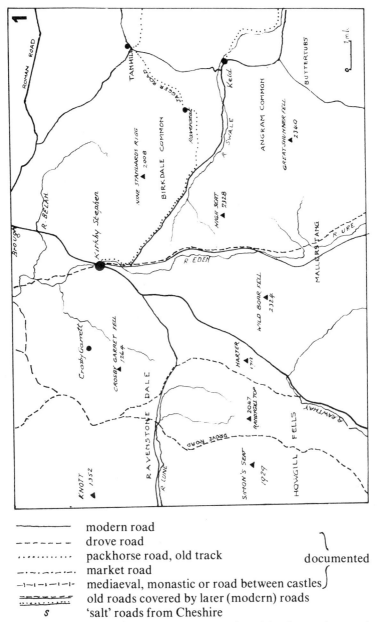

	modern road
— — — — —	drove road
···········	packhorse road, old track
—·—·—·—·—.	market road
—ı—ı—ı—ı—ı—	mediaeval, monastic or road between castles
≈≈≈≈≈≈	old roads covered by later (modern) roads
s	'salt' roads from Cheshire

documented

Roads indicated as documented are mentioned in sixteenth to early nineteenth-century manuscripts or printed sources.

From the county boundary on Lambs Moss, the road drops down across Nateby Common, and by Nateby village to Kirkby Stephen. The whole run of this road forms a fairly direct line between the important castle towns of Barnard Castle, Bowes and Kirkby Stephen (Croglin Castle), avoiding Brough Castle, which would have been approached by the Stainmore road.

At Tan Hill this road is crossed by an equally important ancient way from Richmond to Brough and Appleby. From Richmond to Reeth this is largely the present dale road, going forward up Arkengarthdale and to Tan Hill via Cocker. The old line of the road, however, after passing Arkle Town and Langthwaite, differs considerably from this and is more direct. At half a mile beyond Low Eskeleth a green road takes off to the west on the north side of Whaw Gill and goes in an almost direct line for the junction of Great and Little Punchard Gills, crossing Little Punchard Gill first, over the narrow Tongue End, across Great Punchard Gill and up the north bank of the stream. Passing several lead mines—Routh Level, Fox's Level, Agnes Level and so on—it climbs rapidly on to Punchard Head at Punchard Coal Level.

Here the country changes, the coal level being driven on the Tan Hill Coal, near the base of the Millstone Grit. The Millstone Grit series makes up the massive fells of Water Crag rising to over 2,000 feet OD. The road climbs steeply to the top of the " edge " formed by the outcrop of the lowest grit, this offering dry and firm ground in an area of soft peaty moors. The road runs for some distance on the top of Annaside Edge just reaching 2,000 feet OD. at its highest point, but never much below it, then swings round into the head of William Gill. Here again are more of the Tan Hill coal pits, all around the outcrop.

Over the shoulder of Mirk Fell the road passes Kings Pit colliery and so to Tan Hill. From Tan Hill to the north-west the road is modernised but continues the direct line of this old track. This was the shortest way from Richmond to Brough and Appleby, and in the early days was a very busy track. The collieries at and around Tan Hill belonged to Richmond Castle in the thirteenth and fourteenth centuries, and their coal was sent to the Castle by this road. The steward of the castle accounted yearly for the pits and for the: coal brought from them.

1 Tan Hill, a packmen's and colliers' public house at the centre of a packhorse road system. Coal roads radiate from here into Westmorland and North Yorkshire. The signpost on the right is the Pennine Way sign.

2 A train of packhorses on the Yorkshire moors, from a drawing of 1898.

3   Paving on the Jagger Road
from Tan Hill to Kirkby Stephen at
Ravenseat Ford in Upper Swaledale.

4   Bridge on the Jagger Road at
Ravenseat.

5 'Drovers and their flocks in the North of England' by T. S. Cooper, 1837.

6 Packhorses and driver, from Pyne's *Microcosm,* 1803.

7   The Moor Guide at Spittal on Stainmoor, necessary for the many wild tracks over the extensive moors north of Swaledale, from Walker's *Costume of Yorkshire,* 1814. Spittal on Stainmoor, originally maintained by Marrick Priory, is now only seen as a few foundations.

8   Packhorses, from Pyne's *Microcosm,* 1803.

At a later date the pits belonged to Lady Anne Clifford, and she had coal carried from them by the western part of the same road to Appleby and also some to Whitehaven for the silversmiths there. There is an entry in her diary, " Aug. 1673. Payed the 16 day John Swewell Richd. Browne and other both of Brough and Warcopp for eight score and two loads of coales from my owne pitts in Stainmore at 12d. per load for firing my house at this Appleby Castle." These two roads so far described were busy with pack horses and small carts, until very recent times, distributing the coal from the collieries to the smelt mills, Reeth, Bowes, Brough and Kirkby Stephen and all the country between.

From Tan Hill there is another old road which goes directly down West Stonesdale to Keld and, by the road through Muker and Oxnop Gill, crosses over Askrigg Common to Askrigg and Wensleydale. For a time the part of this road between Askrigg and Keld joining Birkdale to Kirkby Stephen carried Wensleydale knitted goods and wool to the north.

The remaining road of this major group is the old road up Swaledale from Grinton to Muker and Keld, the continuation of which is the Birkdale road just described. As this is the oldest road up the dale, and as all the upper dale is in the ancient parish of Grinton, burials from the villages and houses west of Grinton were carried along it to Grinton church until 1850, when the chapel of ease was built at Muker. From the carriage of folk for burial along this old road it has got the name of the Corpse Way, though for centuries it was the ordinary road for all traffic. From Reeth, the road lies with the modern one as far as Healaugh, beyond which the modern road keeps to the valley bottom. West of Healaugh, the High Lane crosses Barney Beck at the High Bridge, and continues as Morley Gate to Kearton and forward to Blades.

Between Kearton and Blades the old road probably branched, one part keeping along the higher level, the other dropping down by Peat Gate Head to Feetham, then by Brocka Bank to Blades and by Lane End to Smarber. From Smarber to Lodge Green the road kept well up the hillside high above the present road. Crossing Gunnerside Beck to Gunnerside, it then went over the foot of Gunnerside Pasture by Dyke Heads, Shoregill Head and Ivelet Head. Through Calvert Houses and along Ivelet Side it reached the river at or near the present Ramps Holme Bridge, then turned back across the Carrs to Muker. Between Muker and Keld the old road climbed by Kisdon farm on to the high edge of Kisdon Hill, running north along the top of the scar of the Main Limestone to the Skeb Skeugh, where it crossed on to the present road between Thorns Green and Cat Hole.

The lines of these various roads across Stainmore Forest link them directly with the castles at Bowes, Brough, Croglin and Richmond, and with the markets that grew up in their protection. We can say with a high degree of certainty that they have been in use from at least the twelfth century and probably much earlier, and remained in frequent use until well into the 19th. Their very direct course is typical of the pack-horse track, where gradients mattered little and distance counted most. A route well above the wooded and swampy valleys was valued, and wherever possible the track climbed above the scree slopes on to the top of a scar or " edge," and this is well exemplified in the Reeth to Tan Hill road, or the old road between Muker and Keld. These " edge " roads gave firm ground for the path, and afforded a clear look-out over the valley-side woods, useful not only for protection against surprise, but as giving a clearer view of landmarks.

Tan Hill has always been a crossing point of important ways, and hence the inevitable site for an inn. The Tan Hill Inn can probably count many centuries of existence, the breaking stage in the long pack-horse journeys, the refuge at night for travellers overtaken on the moors, and the welcome shelter for the miners at the many small collieries in the moors round about. It must have enjoyed a most varied range of visitors, from the important Baronial servant from one of the castles —the travelling merchant, the pack-horse driver, the collier, the drover—to the hiker and motorist of to-day. It was probably used as the lunch place in many a deer hunt in the time when Stainmore Forest was well preserved. Its importance lies entirely in its key position at this green road intersection.

The road over Stainmore from Bowes to Brough has had a very varied history, first as a Roman road then as a road which for some time led into the Kingdom of Scotland, the boundary lying at Rey Cross. In monastic times the road was in sufficient use for the Spittal on Stainmore, a house of rest and refuge, to be maintained by Marrick Priory, and in later centuries for a Moor Guide to be available there to help travellers across this wild upland.

2 Between Swale and Greta

THE first chapter dealt with the quadrangle of country between Reeth, Kirkby Stephen, Tan Hill and Barras. This chapter looks to a smaller area to the east of it, lying roughly between the valley of Arkengarthdale, the lower Swale, the Roman road from Scotch Corner to Barnard Castle, and the road across Stainmoor.

Green roads are essentially a feature of the higher moorlands, and as one approaches the lowlands with their milder climate and richer soils, enclosure and agriculture have gradually reduced the green roads to walled lanes, then the growth of population and near encroachments of industrial traffic, have converted these into a tangled web of second class roads, with none of their original character to be recognised, beyond their general direction and a few place names. On the east side of the Arkle Beck, however, there still remains a wild moorland—the old " New Forest " created by the Norman lords of Richmond Castle, and for some centuries preserved by them for hunting.

Mining has for many centuries been the principal occupation and its population has tended to dwindle rather than increase. In consequence of this there are still many ancient green roads to be traced, though most have now deteriorated into bridle tracks, not too well marked on the higher ground.

During the early centuries after the Norman conquest, when the green roads were probably experiencing their busiest traffic, the relative importance of many places was very different from what it is now. Gilling, Ravensworth, Hartforth, Newsham, were all important centres, declining as Bowes, Barnard Castle and Richmond grew. In Anglian times, before the Normans, Gilling was the central meeting place of the Wapontake, and gave its name to the divisions which are still used in many administrative departments, Gilling East and Gilling West. Many early roads and tracks, therefore, tend to centre on Gilling.

In the monastic period, Jervaulx and Coverham Abbeys had

land in Hartforth and many other manors around, and maintained a traffic between them and the parent abbeys. The foresters of the New Forest had their granges and houses, and the miners were licensed as early as the twelfth century to work at many places in the forest, so that again tracks were made between places which are now hardly more than names upon a map.

From Barnard Castle, which became an important market at an early date, there are many roads to the south-west, some of which come within this present survey. Probably the oldest which must be mentioned, although now modernised, through all this area, is the one which goes to Langthwaite in Arkengarthdale. From Barnard Castle it goes due south to the Roman road between Greta Bridge and Bowes, part of this old line still being a footpath.

South of the main road, it continues by Timpton Hill, then by a rather irregular way to the west by Bowfield and to Thwaite Beck. Between Timpton Hill and the road beyond Thwaite Beck there is an old boundary line which now marks the former line of the old road. The road climbs quickly over Hill Top and West Hope Moor to cross Stang at nearly 1,700 feet OD. then descends rapidly by Stang Side into Arkengarthdale. Formerly this road crossed the present road near the *C.B. Inn,* and continued the same line on the west side of Reeth Low Moor to Feetham, crossed the Swale there and over Whitaside and Summerlodge Moor and the Fleak to Askrigg and Bainbridge.

It is generally thought that this is the line of a Roman road continuing the one over Cam from Ribblesdale. For many long years lead and lead ore was carried by it from Swaledale and Arkengarthdale to the market at Barnard Castle, and down the Tees to Yarm where it could be shipped to the south.

From the *Hill Top Inn* on this road there is an ancient and still green road turning sharply off to the east to West Hope. After crossing the beck the road goes due south-east and in quarter of a mile branches, the east branch going through East Hope, Haythwaite and Bragg House, to Barningham. The south-east branch climbs the hill to the east of Hope Edge and High Band, aiming directly for How Tallon, the great tumulus on the skyline at the summit of Newsham Moor.

Just after crossing Woodclose Gill head, and at about 1,250 feet OD. the track again branches, the left fork keeping along the contour along Barningham Moor side, past Badger Way Stoop, to Newsham Moor Lane. Crossing this lane the track becomes more and more of a true lane turning southward along the crest of Gayles Moor and two miles beyond Newsham Moor Lane becoming Cordilleras Lane down to Marske. This is an ancient trade way, as its name Badger Way indicates, and would be the quickest way between Marske and Barnard Castle. South of Marske the continuation is marked by the road over to Leyburn and Middleham. The Cordilleras Lane portion has, of course, been straightened and walled at the enclosure of Marske Moor in 1809.

Returning to the branch at Woodclose Gill Head, the western part crosses the ridge about a third of a mile west of How Tallon, then drops to the head of Arndale Springs and so along Arndale Beck side, keeping well up on the edge of Hallgate Moor to West House, Hallgate and Helwith and then either to Marske or Marrick, there being tracks to both. Near West House this road crosses another ancient way, coming from Arkle Town and Langthwaite across country to Newsham with a branch to Gayles.

From Arkengarthdale there are many miners' tracks up to the Windegg Mines, from which the Moresdale Road runs east along Moresdale Ridge, past Stony Man or St. Andrew's Cross, joining the road that comes from Langthwaite, by Booze and up the west side of Slie Gill. All the length of Meresdale Ridge there are splendid views across Kexwith Moor and up to the Stang, on the north, and over Hurst and Marrick Moors and across Swaledale to the south. This is one of the very fine moorland ridge ways, most of which are very ancient, often prehistoric. Beyond Kexwith the road crosses Holgate or Hallgate beck and, keeping due east, makes for Rake Gate on Rake Beck and forward to the Stone Man or Tumulus, on Gayles Moor. From here Stone Man Lane leads to Gayles.

The persistence of the term " gate " along this road, and the standing stones or " stone men " which mark it, are important evidence of its antiquity. From Kexwith there is another old road, north-east across Hallgate Moor to Long Green Gate at the very head of Rake Beck, where the road enters a walled lane and, as Moor Lane, continues for three miles in a nearly straight line for Newsham.

Again, the straightening and walling of this lane and conversion to " Moor Road " would be the work of the Enclosure

Commissioners in the early years of the nineteenth century, before which time there were a multitude of tracks alongside, the traffic shifting from one as it got too deep and rutty and making a new one on the hardest ground near at hand. In many cases the name Hollowgate, and Hollow-way or Holloway, indicates such an old pack-horse road, and it is possible that some of the many Hallgates and Holgates are variants of the same word, altered through the centuries.

Many place names have suffered a wonderful change in the course of making the original survey. The Ordnance Survey was carried through in the first place by the Royal Ordnance Corps, largely centred in the south, and we must picture the soldiers of southern origin, and the officers with them, collecting the local names from the natives—there would be much puzzling over the sound of the dialect, and many attempts to find an English word that looked something like what the local name had sounded.

It is in this way that some of our queerest names originate, and as the surveyors mapped more and more sheets in one area, they would get used to thinking of, and putting a wide variety of sounds into, variants of one word. In this way, many of the respectable looking Halgates, Holgates, Jigger Lane, Jagger Lane, and so on have achieved a queer variety of spellings from a few originals.

Starting from the present high road between Marske and Richmond on the north side of the Swale, Jagger Lane, now only remaining in fragments, its full line being partly obscured, crosses Richmond Out Moor, then as a walled lane continues north east between Black Plantation and Gilling Wood and on to Hartforth. The road is an important boundary, a strong argument for its great antiquity. At the corner of Black Plantation—and notice once again the place name Black associated with boundaries—the boundaries of Easby, Gilling and Kirkby Ravensworth meet.

Nearly parallel to Jagger Lane on the north-west side is Sturdy House Lane going to Kirkby Ravensworth. Throughout its length this is enclosed by typical early nineteenth century walling, in long ruled lengths, and its original nature is hardly preserved anywhere. Beyond Hartforth, Jagger Lane can still be traced in great part as far as Melsonby, probably only a first stage in a much longer journey now not completely traceable.

This Jagger Lane falls into place in a wider pattern of salt and coal roads. During all the Middle Ages and even until the eighteenth century, salt was essential for preserving the winter stock of meat, and it was a perennial market. From an early date saltpans, where brine was evaporated from sea water, had flourished on the north-east coast and much of Durham and North Yorkshire was served from them. In the fourteenth and fifteenth centuries there was a great salt industry also in south east Durham, with saltpans around Seaton Carew and Hartlepool, and also on the Yorkshire side of the Tees near Coatham, and from all these places Salters' tracks penetrate North Yorkshire.

As the coal mining industry developed new saltpans tended to be concentrated around the rivers, which were used for the coal export, as coal could be obtained there at the cheapest rates. The old pans declined. By the seventeenth century the rivers Bluthe, Tyne and Wear were the centres of the salt trade, and Sunderland became important. From Sunderland there is a well known pack-horse road to the south-west, the Salter's Track, becoming known in its southern part as the Darnton (Darlington) Trod. Branches from this served much of south-west Durham and Teesdale.

From Darlington it continues south-west and crosses the Tees by fords in the vicinity of Stapleton or by the old Tees Bridge, then continues in a fairly straight line to Melsonby. From here we have already traced it to Richmond Out Moor, but there are many branches from it—Melsonby to Kirkby Ravensworth then by Gayles to Marske, Marrick, Reeth and Upper Swaledale as already described; and from Melsonby to Richmond by Gilling. From Richmond Out Moor the Jagger Road continues by High and Low Applegarth to the ford over the Swale near Collier Hag, then mounts the south bank through Strand Wood, Scarcote Wood and across the modern road to the road over Middlemoor, called Green Lane. This part of the road was straightened and walled at the enclosure of Hudswell fields in 1808, and a branch lane to the east was given at that time the amusing name of Notagreen Lane.

The Jagger road goes forward by Waithwath Bank, where it is joined by a direct road from Richmond Bridge. This would be used when the river was too high for the ford to be safe. South of this junction the road is again an important boundary between parishes and also between Poor Law Unions and Rural Districts. It crosses Barden Fell between Half-penny House and Hipswell Moor, and passes Hartleap Well, commemorated by Wordsworth. The road is, of course, now the ordinary road to Bellerby and Leyburn, largely altered and remade when it was constituted a Turnpike by an Act of 1751.

Along with salt, a certain amount of coal was brought into the Richmond district by this road, and in the eighteenth and nineteenth century some salt was brought along a second road from Yarm, where it was imported from Scotland. There are green roads from many sides to Yarm, formerly the principal point for shipment for North Yorkshire and South-east Durham, for lead and corn destined for London or abroad.

In the land between the Swale and Ure which lies east of Askrigg there are very few green roads. The old tracks between Grinton and Redmire, and Grinton and Leyburn, have been completely modernised and only a few ways remain in unmade condition, these mainly connected with the wide-spread area of coalpits making up the Preston Moor collieries. There is one section of unchanged road from Preston-under-Scar going up the moor to Broomber Rigg, starting as a walled lane, then turning as an open track due west by Cobscar Smelt Mill until it joins the Grinton Road above Redmire quarries. Another similar road runs north-east from the Grinton to Leyburn road on Preston Moor, down the north side of Stainton Moor Beck and so to Stainton, forward to Downham and along the hill crest to Hudswell and so to Richmond.

An old track, now a footpath, only goes north-west up Apedale and over Whitaside Moor, coming down to Whitaside Mine, and was no doubt used principally by miners between the Apedale and Whitaside groups of mines. The track, however, continues to the Askrigg to Healaugh road and would be a convenient short cut from Redmire over to that part of Swaledale. The remaining few tracks in this area are access ways to the various lead and coal mines, and are now out of use. In the lower and richer farming ground in the eastern part of the area nearly all tracks are now lost in the abundant lanes and secondary roads which link almost every village with Richmond, Leyburn or Middleham.

In this area, then, there is a basic structure of early tracks, many of which link up with the Salt roads and with old ad-

ministrative centres and markets at Gilling, Kirkby Ravensworth, Barnard Castle, Leyburn, and so on. On this there
is superposed a web of miners' tracks leading to and from
remote mines and to the newer markets. The disentangling
of this mixed web will provide unlimited enjoyment for the
keen walker who loves to get away from modern roads with
their burden of traffic.

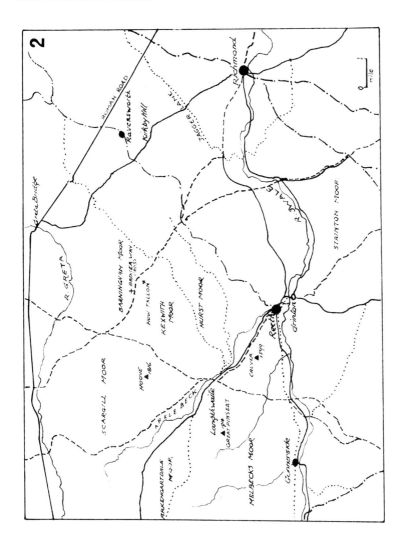

3   West of Hawes

FROM Brough and Kirkby Stephen old roads found a way
into Yorkshire by Mallerstang, a way which was guarded
by Pendragon Castle.   This is all part of the pre-Roman forest
of Reged where, later, King Arthur is said by some to have
been born, son to the king Uther Pendragon of Pendragon in
Mallerstang.   The Mallerstang roads bring us down to the
complex of valley heads and high fells between Hawes, Sedbergh and Ingleton, in and across which there is an abundance of green roads and tracks of many ages—Roman military
ways, later drove roads and still later peat and accommodation
roads.   A great post-road from London to Kendal was well
used for many long years, from Wensleydale going by the
Moorcock, Garsdale and Sedbergh.

The recent roads have in some parts used the line of an
older one for a distance, but on the whole the Turnpikes of the
late eighteenth century and early nineteenth have avoided the
difficult gradients of the older roads and have cut for them-
selves new lines nearer the valley bottoms.

As the south eastern boundary to the present area we can
take the main road from Ingleton to Hawes by Ribblehead and
Widdale which is the Richmond to Lancaster Turnpike Trust
road.   From Ingleton to Chapel-le-dale this is a new line, the
part from Chapel-le-dale to Cam Fell corner being roughly on
the line of the Roman road from Bainbridge to Casterton.   In
Garsdale the road from Sedbergh to Garsdale Head is only
approximately on the line of an older road.   The road from
Hawes through Mallerstang to Kirkby Stephen is almost all
new.   Up the Lune valley the older road runs along the fell
side a short distance above the nineteenth century Turnpike,
though that in parts uses a Roman road as foundation.   In
Dentdale the modern road is " improved " on the older line.

If we turn to old roads which remain largely unaltered,
there is plenty of choice in every direction.   The road which is
most like those already described on the Stainmore Forest and
Tan Hill, is the old road from Hawes to Kirkby Stephen.   From

Hawes to Appersett the old and present roads coincide in great part, but it is not clear just where the old road crossed the river.   Less than a mile beyond Appersett, near Collier Holme, the present Turnpike road bends to the west while an old lane goes forward in a direct line up Cotter End, the spur between Cotterdale and the main valley.

This old lane was the main road until the Turnpike road was made in 1825; it rises rapidly to the top of Cotter Clints, the shelf-like outcrop of the limestone which forms a nearly level terrace running for miles along the fell side.   The old road keeps close to the edge, just along the top of the scar, affording most inspiring views down Garsdale and across the Baugh Fell — Wild Boar Fell group of hills.   This old road is called the *High Way* in this part of its course, but in Mallerstang for a short way it takes the name of *Street*, both being very ancient names. The road passes by High Dike Farm, High Way, and Horse Paddock, with a by road going down the scar from High Dike to Lunds church.   From the church there is another steep road climbing back to the High Way and rejoining it at High Hall near Washer Gill.   These compound names in *High*— attached to so many old farms and buildings—speak of the age of the High Way itself.

The Horse Paddock is especially interesting as a relic of what at one time was a common feature.   It is a walled and irregular enclosure of a few acres, forming now a detached portion of the parish of High Abbotside.   It was a halting place for pack horse trains, where a long journey could be broken at night, the packs stored in safe buildings and the ponies turned out into a safe enclosure.   Similar " stage houses " were provided along most long distance pack-horse routes, but most have now disappeared or are only to be re-cognised in the wayside inns like *Tan Hill*, or a farm house like Dale Head on Penyghent side.

The High Way crosses Hell Gill at the fine Hell Gill Bridge, then drops slowly down to the valley bottom at Mal-lerstang, crosses the river at a ford and proceeds to Pendragon Castle, then forward by Lammerside Castle and Wharton Hall to Croglin Castle and Kirkby Stephen.   This is the road by which Lady Anne Clifford travelled from Skipton to Appleby in 1663, as described in her diary where she says: " and the next day I went over Cotter, which I lately repaired, and I came into the Pendragon's Castle. . ." It was thus an ancient road in the seventeenth century, and evidently then in need of repair. There are short roads connecting it with Garsdale Head, now mainly represented by field paths.

There is a very ancient road out of Cotterdale which climbs nearly west from the hamlet, crosses High Abbotside at 1,750 feet OD., and comes down to the High Way at High Dike, which was formerly a drovers' inn. A little beyond High Dike the road branches down to Lund's Church to which, for many generations the folk of Cotterdale were carried for burial, this old track often being called the Corpse Road.

Garsdale offers many short lengths of old road, and green roads mount the fells on each side of the dale to the peat allotments and moorland pasture, but the only road we need detail here is the one called the *Galloway Gate*. This is a true green road, and very ancient. It leaves Garsdale at Knows Foot Bridge just below the railway station at Garsdale Junction, and climbs the southern fell up Garsdale Common on to Cowgill Head at about 1,760 feet OD. Keeping a little below this level around Pikes Edge and to the western side of Great Knoutberry at about 1,700 feet OD., it then turns down Monkey Beck Grains, past Dent station to Cowgill Chapel and so by the north bank of the Dee to Dent.

From the head of Monkey Beck there is a continuation of the contour road which goes round Dent Fell to the head of Arten Gill, where it is joined by a similar road from the head of Dentdale. By the east side of Widdale Fell, this road now drops down into Widdale and crosses the beck at an old bridge at Widdale Foot, into the present road line. This road around Dent Fell is called the *Driving Road* although never used for " driving " with carriage and pair and most likely a corruption of *Droving* road. It provides some of the finest views down Dentdale and its surroundings that are to be obtained anywhere in the district.

The Galloway Gate has a double importance—it is the old main road out of Dentdale into Mallerstang and by the high way to Kirkby Stephen, and was regularly traversed by pack-horse trains going to and from that market; it also served the extensive pits of the Garsdale Colliery. Along the whole of its length small branch roads take off to the various shafts, in fact in its long rise out of Dentdale up to Pikes Edge it is called Coal Road in old deeds and manuscripts. The Galloway Gate gets its name partly from the "galloways" used as pack-horses for transport of the coal and other goods and partly as a branch of the Galloway Gate which was an ancient drove road for Scottish ·cattle from Galloway.

Garsdale Colliery has a long history and was worked for a few centuries until the coming of the railway brought better and cheaper coal into the area. Most of the workings were reached by small shafts where the winding was done by a hand-turned "jack roller." The grass grown shaft heaps are very numerous and indicate clearly the very wide former extent of the concern.

From Dent there are two other pack-horse roads of great age and interest. The one that is now least used but very attractive, leaves the old road on the south of the Dee at Deepdale foot, and from Dike Hall rises rapidly as a walled lane up the northwest shoulder on to Great Wold. After climbing to over 1,600 feet OD., it becomes an unfenced road and soon mounts on to the firm, dry limestone terrace that forms the ridge of Great Wold. Turning more to the south it crosses a highest point at just over 1,700 feet OD., and then drops to the head of Force Gill. In this part of the road the old name of *Craven's Old Way* is given on some of the older maps while in the dispute over the Dent-Newby boundary it is called *Craven's Wath* or *Little Craven's Wald,* the road from Dent to Ingleton.

Down Little Dale it reaches the hamlet of Winterscales then keeps on the lower flank of Whernside past Ivescar and Bruntscar to Ellerbeck, turning abruptly at the latter point down the hillside to Chapel-le-dale. From Chapel-le-dale it continues as the walled green road on the west side of the Greta to Beezleys, and down the tongue of land between the two sets of falls to Ingleton. This part of the road from Chapel-le-dale to Beezleys may in fact be much older and be part of the Roman road from Bainbridge to Casterton, being a direct continuation of the Camm Fell road line.

A rather similar fell-side road leaves Dent by Flinters Gill and climbs on to the breast of Crag Hill, again finding an approximate contour way round the north flank, turning south in a great curve round the head of Blea Gills, into the top of Deepdale, where it joins another road that has followed the

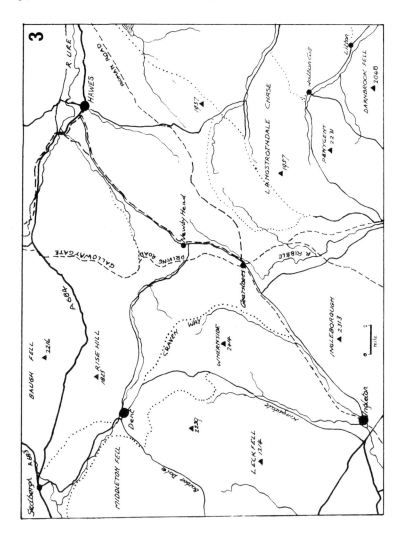

west side of Deepdale from Dent. From the head of Flinter-gill to the head of Deepdale this is now a walled green road, the walling dating only from about 1860, but it follows the line of a much older track which in parts can be seen on one side or other of the present line.

The road then goes forward down Kingsdale, past Thornton Force to Thornton and forward to Lancaster. Like the Galloway Gate, this road besides through market traffic, served many small coal pits on the flanks of Crag Hill. It was also a " high road " alternative to the Deepdale road, for the coal traffic from Ingleton colliery into Dentdale. There is another green road from Dent and Gawthrop through Barbondale to Barbon, and so on to the Kirkby Lonsdale road. This is probably the best known of these roads at the present time.

A green road of less importance, and probably never much more than a peat and high-pasture accommodation road, rises from Barbon on to the shoulder of Gragareth, passing Bull Pot farm, then keeping on the west side, just below the summit ridge. It passes below the brow of Crag Hill and drops into Flinters Gill but, except at the two ends, it is now almost forgotten.

We are fortunate in having some account of the traffic along these roads from the pen of Adam Sedgwick, the geologist, to whom the memorial stands in the middle of Dent village. Sedgwick was born in 1785 and tells us in his writings that it was the greatest joy of his childhood to talk with the older men of the dale and hear their stories of dales life as it was lived in their youth. At a later time in his life he collected most of these memories, and the information so obtained spans the period from about 1740 to after 1800. Much of this was incorporated in a little book with the unpromising title, *A Memorial by the Trustees of Cowgill Chapel, with a preface and appendix on the climate, history and dialects of Dent* by Adam Sedgwick, Ll.D. Privately printed. Cambridge 1868. There is also a *Supplement to the Memorial by the Trustees . . . etc.* printed in 1870.

Speaking of his childhood he says that at that time, about 1790, all external produce was brought into Dent by carriers from Hawes, Kendal and Kirkby Lonsdale. Some women as well as men were engaged in the carrying trade, and he speaks of a Mrs. Beckett and her daughter Peggy who were carriers to Kendal. They went to Kendal every Friday for the Saturday

market, returning very late on Saturday night, and were generally preferred to the men carriers because of their greater skill
in choosing provisions and matching drapery goods.

Dent was a busy place with a population twice that of Sedbergh, and much greater than at present. It was widely known
as a producer of wool, which was partly carded and manufac-
tured for home use in Dent; it became better known, however,
for its large production of stockings and gloves knitted from
imported dressed wool and worsted. " The weekly transport of
the goods which kept this trade alive was effected, first by trains
of pack-horses, and afterwards by small carts fitted for mountain
work." Later machine spun worsted was brought into the dale
*and the knit worsted stockings were the greatest article of export
from the Northern Dales. Such bcame the importance of this
export, about the middle of last century, that Government Agents
were placed at Kirkby Lonsdale, Kendal and Kirkby Stephen,
during the ' Seven Years' War ' for the express purpose of securing for the use of the English army (then in service on the Con-
tinent) the worsted stockings knit by the hands of the Dalesmen;
and in this trade Dent had an ample share.*

It will be noticed that he says knit by the hands of the
dalesmen, and readers will remember that in Walker's picture
of the Knitters of Hawes, everyone, men, women and children,
is knitting.

Sedgwick says that in the last century (the eighteenth) another source of trade and industry was the coal-works, coal
being brought to Dent from Garsdale collieries, and also some
coal from the pits on Crag Hill was carried to Kendal by pack-
horse. This coal was very thin, only seven or eight inches, but
was of good quality and was specially liked by the whitesmiths.
The roads used by the pack horses and the small carts are vividly
described by Sedgwick:

*I remember some roads in Dent so narrow that there was
barely room for one of the little country carts to pass along them;
and they were so little cared for, that, in the language of the
country the way " was as rough as the beck staens."*

*I remember, too, when the carts and the carriages were of
the rudest character; moving on wheels which did not revolve
about their axle; but the wheels and their axle were joined so as
to revolve together. Four strong pegs of wood fixed in a cross-
beam under the cart embraced the axle-tree, which revolved*

9   Rey Cross on Stainmoor, erected in AD 946 at the side of the Roman Road from Bowes to Brough.

11 The road up West Stonesdale from Swaledale to Tan Hill. For some centuries shepherds and drovers were the most numerous users of these roads. *(B. Unne)*

12 Road menders on the Askrigg to Muker road, at the top of Oxnop Gill, from Walker's *Costume of Yorkshire,* 1814.

13　The road between Hawes and Buckden by Langstrothdale at Fleet Moss, formerly a green road. *(B. Unne)*

14　The Roman road from Bainbridge over Cam Fell, with Ingleborough in the distance. This green road is now well used by walkers. *(B. Unne)*

15   Mastiles Lane, a thirteenth century monastic road from Fountains Abbey. It was a very busy drove road in the seventeenth, eighteenth and early nineteenth centuries, and was walled about 1760. *(Yorkshire Dales National Park)*

16   One of several cross bases on Mastiles Lane. This is where two monastic tracks Trougate and Mastiles Lane, cross near Malham Tarn. Trougate is now used by the Pennine Way.

17   Clapper bridge and ford in Crummack Dale near Austwick. The smaller bridge is on a branch track. These stones are Horton Flags from the Helwith Bridge quarries, and are found on many old tracks in the dales.

18   Peat cutters in Langstrothdale with a typical clog-wheeled cart of the kind used on many of the green roads, from Walker's *Costume of Yorkshire*, 1814.

19   Top Mere Road climbing out
of Kettlewell in Upper Wharfedale.
(Yorkshire Dales National Park).

20   An early eighteenth-century
guide post on the very old green road
from Middleham to Hawes.

*between the pegs, as the cart was dragged on, with a horrible
amount of friction that produced a creaking noise, in the ex-
pressive language of the Dales called* JYKING.

*The friction was partially relieved by frequent doses of tar,
administered to the pegs from a ram's horn which hung behind
the cart. Horrible were the creakings and jykings which set all
teeth on edge while the turf carts or coal-carts were dragged
from the mountains to the houses of the dalesmen in the hamlets
below.*

The demand for coal was very insistent in the eighteenth
century and, until the coming of the railways later in the nineteenth century, it was carried all over the countryside by the
trains of pack-horses and small carts, from every outcrop that
was at all useable. In 1820 a traveller in Craven says, when
travelling by horse from Kirkby Lonsdale to Ingleton " the
number of small carts laden with coal, and each dragged by
one sorry horse that we met was surprising to a stranger. Many
of the small farmers between Kirkby Lonsdale and Kendal earn
half their bread with carrying coals, during most part of the
year, from the pits at Ingleton and Burton-in-Lonsdale to Kendal
and the neighbouring places for fuel and burning lime in order
to manure their land." Almost every outcrop, large or small,
shows evidence of working, and tracks are still to be seen linking
them with the nearest of the old green roads, or with lime-kilns
which in turn link to the roads.

From Arten Gill there is a road forward to Newby Head,
now part of the macadamised and modern road group, which
was in constant use for centuries in connection with the ancient
weekly market at Gearstones. This market was held every
Wednesday until about 1870, for the sale of corn and oatmeal.
In the early nineteenth century as many as 20 or 30 carts a week
came to it from Wensleydale, laden with grain, and trains of
pack-horses attended from all the dales, travelling by the green
roads, some of which have been mentioned.

Only the principal roads have been described so far. In
addition to these there are many shorter lengths of purely local
road, mainly very old and ill-defined trackways, converted into
walled roads by the enclosure awards. Such, for instance, is the
Turbary road from Mason Gill which goes up Ireby Fell, then
by Thorney Rigg, past Jingling Pot and on the top of Shout
Scar, turning up by Bull Pot to the Turbary Pasture.

Near Hawes there is a group of colliery roads, the best

marked being the *Hearne Coal Road* from Hardraw by Blea Pot
and the west side of Bleakthwaite Beck to Fossdale Moss and
the line of coal pits which extends below Pickersett Edge from
the head of Bleakthwaite Beck round to Fossdale, forming the
Hearne and West Pit collieries. Cotterdale pits are on the same
coal seam with a green road to them branching off from the
Hearne road on the summit of Blue Bell Hill. Similar roads are
found all over the area leading mainly to coal pits in the north-
western part of the Dales, to lead mines in other parts, and to
peat grounds and lime-kilns everywhere.

4   Bowland Forest

WEST of the Ribble, south of the Kirkby Lonsdale to Settle road, there is a large area in which few green roads are found. A great part of this area is Bowland Forest and part of Mewith Forest. During the centuries in which many of the tracks we are studying were being made, this was carefully secluded country with the minimum access for common folk who might disturb or poach the deer and other game.

There are few roads across Bowland. Even today there are really only two main roads with a few branches from them. The best known is, of course, the road from Clitheroe by which the buses now reach to Slaidburn, a road which continues beyond Slaidburn by climbing up to Tosside then descending to Wigglesworth and Long Preston. An ancient and much used way from Clitheroe to Lancaster comes over Waddington Fell, by Walloper Well, crossing the other road near Dunsop Bridge into the valley leading to the spectacular Trough of Bowland and so to Wyresdale. Both these roads are now entirely modernised but patches and shreds of the older tracks are still to be found alongside them in many parts of their run.

From Slaidburn four roads radiate between N.W. and N.E., the least altered of them being a Salters' Gate, which leaves Slaidburn as a lane on the west side of Croasdale. When the last farm at Ramsclough is passed, the track continues up Croasdale on to the ridge of Salter Fell. It continues on the high edge which makes the north east flank of the deep valley of the River Roeburn, and goes through the Higher Salter Close. From High Salter the track becomes a good road making directly for Hornby Castle and then to the crossing of the Lune at Gressingham. The other roads from Slaidburn are the one up the Hodder and over Lythe Fell to High Bentham, and another from Slaidburn to Clapham Station, now a popular motor run across Bowland Knotts.

The road from Slaidburn to Long Preston has two branches not far from Slaidburn, one down Holden Clough to Bolton-by-Bowland and Sawley, and a more direct road to Grindleton and Chatburn. Both these are very ancient ways but they are now modernised out of all recognition. East of the Ribble there is the mass of Pendle Hill and Pendle Forest, rich in footpaths, and the piece of country between Pendle and the Craven Hills. Toward Barnoldswick there are many tracks but the pattern is much complicated by the abundance of lanes between farms and small hamlets, many of which may be very old, but are not really a part of ancient green roads as we are defining them.

One lane is an ancient way without doubt, from Gisburn to Colne, south from Gisburn by two short lengths of footpath onto Coal Pit lane. This goes by Bonny Blacks, which significantly is on a boundary line, and then forward on to Ridge of Weets. Here the lane is left for a length of footpath linking it with the continuation which is a walled lane, Gisburn Old Road. This way has long been superseded by the road through Barnoldswick. Salterforth is a ford on one of the great saltways, making towards Skipton and traceable through much of its length.

In the country south west of Skipton there is a bewildering maze of lanes and secondary roads, perhaps most developed in the patch between Keighley, Skipton and Colne. There are some very direct roads which stick to an ancient pattern, going along the hillsides with only a slight diversion where it is necessary to avoid an upstanding hill summit, or to get to a good ford. Two examples of these direct roads are sufficient, little of them now being in fact green roads. From Skipton to Colne two old roads go by Carleton, one taking the way over Elslack Moor and the head of Lothersdale, and the other is a little to the east of it on lower ground.

The second goes from Earby to Glusburn and Crosshills. The unravelling of this great tangle of tracks could provide a hobby for many summers and would lead one into many quaint nooks and corners of the earliest phases of industrial England, when wool and cotton was put out to cottages and farms to be spun and woven and the pack-horse man was the commonest traveller on this multitude of tracks. Peat roads, quarry roads and accommodation ways on to the upland grazing add their quota to the confusion, but all lead to the grand country of the higher moors.

In this area of Bowland and south west of Skipton there are Roman roads which in part have become modern secondary roads or lanes, but which in part are represented by green tracks or footpaths. One such road through Bowland, made

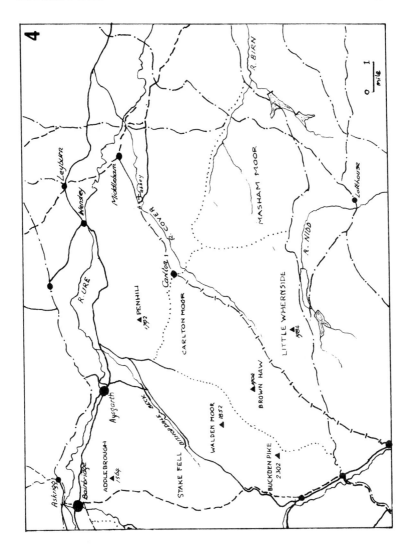

by the Romans, goes northward from Ribchester towards Penrith in the Vale of Eden. At Ribchester on the Ribble the road from Ilkley, coming by Skipton, Elslack and Whalley, crosses the river at Little Town to enter the Roman city of Bremetannacvm from the east. The road from Manchester via Blackburn comes up from the south and the northern road goes half a mile from Ribchester to Cherry Yate then makes a straight course for two and a half miles N.N.W. to Dale House on Longridge Fell. Here it turns to the N.E. and has a length as straight as a ruler for six and a half miles, making exactly for Slaidburn and Newton.

At its second contact with the river Hodder near Newton, it turns more to the north across the foothill slopes of Burn Fell as far as Low Fell in Croasdale, two miles N.W. of Slaidburn. For all this way from the Ribble to Newton great lengths of the road are still in use and the gaps are generally bridged by footpaths. From near Newton to the Croasdale valley the line is known but is not now marked by any track. At Low Fell the character of the road changes, being no longer on a ruled line, but wandering slightly to meet the changing contour of the valley side up Hard Hill Top towards Salter Fell. This part was in use for many centuries as part of the Salters' Way to Hornby, already described.

Just before reaching Guide Hill, the very curious high mound on the shoulder of Salter Fell, the Roman road turns off to the North and soon becomes visible as a track making down the east side of the headwaters of the river Hindburn in a straight line for Old Wennington, making a slight diversion east to cross the Wenning near West End. From Old Wennington the road goes to Casterton and is largely used thence by the old road north through Borrans and Applegarth, which runs to the east of the modern Sedbergh road. From Middleton Hall there are old lanes to Ingmire Hall and High Branthwaite and then the delightful road on the slope of the Howgill Fells, by Bland's Gill, Gate Side (a significant road name) and Fairmile Gate to cross the Lune at Low Borrowbridge to the Roman fort there.

Returning to Bowland a few ancient ways are still to be found partly represented by footpaths, short lengths of green road and rough lanes, though they are by no means abundant. One such track leaves Rathmell and climbs to Whelpstone Lodge, formerly called Ragged Hall, at the end of an

old lane called Old Oliver Lane. This name is probably connected with very early iron making, using ores from some of
the Millstone Grit shales and making iron in a bloomery. The
bloom was hammered into good wrought iron with a foot ham-
mer called an " oliver." This place name—e.g. near Cowling,
and above Middleton in Wharfedale, and other places—is associated with iron making activities. From Whelpstone Lodge
the lane degenerates to a footpath under the edge of Whelpstone Crag and down to the head of Bailey Lane, a green road
from Tosside to Clough Hall. Near Hindley Head there is a
branch track to the west past the site of Bottoms on Bottoms
Beck and by Cocklick End to Hasgill Beck, then as a green
road down to Stocks in Bowland (now submerged in the Stocks
Reservoir).

From Stocks an old road by Grange continues by Hollins
and Phynis to Slaidburn, or an alternative track goes from
Grange to Slaidburn by Hammerton Hall. This long track
was more a connection between Rathmell, and possibly Settle,
and Stocks-in-Bowland, than with Slaidburn, to which the road
via Tosside would be more direct.

It might be convenient at this point to bring in a rather
fine track associated with the Ingleborough mass connecting
Clapham and Hawes. This leaves Clapham as Long Lane and
by Long Scar reaches the wide area of limestone upland called
Sulber. Crossing Sulber the track goes down to the very
ancient farm of Borrins to Selside. From Selside the track
crosses the Ribble by a ford and so to Birkwith and High
Birkwith then to the ancient pack-horse bridge at the head of
Ling Gill. There is a tablet set in the bridge with an in-
scription " Anno 1765. This bridge was repaired at the charge
of the whole West Riding."

From Ling Gill Bridge the green road, now nearly ob-
literated, makes due north for Cam Fell End and there joins
the Roman road across Cam Fell and Wether Fell to Bainbridge. However at the head of Sleddale the old road, now
entirely modernised, takes down the east side of the valley to
Gayle and Hawes. At Selside and at Low Birkwith there are
branches from this old road to Gearstones on Ribblehead, for
many centuries the site of an important market and a meeting
place for drovers. From Gearstones many drove roads diverge,
but most of them have already been described in other chapters.

5 The Heart of Craven

THE area at the heart of Craven in the upper reaches of the Wharfe, Aire and Ribble, is not very rich in important green roads to which a definite history can be attached. There are, however, a number of ancient ways crossing from one valley to another which are often links in roads which in times past served as highways between far distant places, going by routes which have now almost dropped out of use. There are in addition a large number of short mine and peat roads from the valleys to the fells, which provide now a most pleasant access to the higher ground, and frequently lead to footpaths which carry one forward to the next dale.

Some of the old through roads have in part been absorbed in modern roads, but fragments still remain in their old un-metalled or partly metalled, grassed conditioned, and provided the title " green roads " is not too rigidly interpreted their old lines can still be followed almost in their entirety.

Some of the higher paths across the fells, and particularly such as keep fairly well along the valley edges at a high level, may be of prehistoric date, but generally the oldest recog-nisable roads are those made by the Romans, and of these there is at least one good example in the area. The Roman road from Bainbridge to Ilkley is traceable in part, particularly near Buckden. Coming south from the camp at Bainbridge, the early part of the road is easily recognised, but nothing certain can be traced over the top of the Stake Allotment. The old green road called Busk Lane continues Carpley Green road beyond Carpley Green by a remarkable straight line for half a mile or more. It then makes a big bend towards the west, coming back to a straight line across Busk Moss. It is not until the head of Bishopdale that the road again becomes cer-tain and here, across the wide extent of peaty ground, the road is very straight, with the Bishopdale road turning off about the middle. On old maps it is called Causeway. The peaty ground also is Causeway Moss, and this name is found in the fifteenth century in the boundaries of Langstrothdale Chase.

This ancient name suggests a metalled and firm road such as a Roman road would provide.

Near Cray High Bridge the road coming down from Causeway Moss makes a sharp bend to the west, as Blackstone Lane, and at this point an old overgrown road continues the due south line on top of the limestone scar, keeping to firm, well-drained ground. This is the Roman road which, opposite Cray, swings a little to the south west, but keeps on top of the limestone shelf and is called in this part, Buckden Rake. At the top of Rakes Wood it turns again towards Buckden, and makes a rapid, straight line descent through the wood to the village.

In parts this road is a clear rock-cut line. Sometimes it is partially cut in the scar and built up on the outside. All the way is firm and well made. It crosses the Buckden Gill by a ford and fragments can be traced through the fields to Starbotton and Kettlewell, a little above the present road. Further down the dale part of its line is used by the modern roads, so need not be described here.

The head of Wharfedale and its tributary Littondale presents a curious physiographic feature in the way in which the valleys, including some of the smaller tributaries, swing round through nearly a semicircle, into the broad depression at the head of Ribblesdale. At the very head of Wharfe, Oughtershaw Beck starts as a stream flowing north-east, then east, then south-east, and in its early north-east course it is only continuing a valley in that direction through which Cam Beck flows down to the Ribble. There is a similar crescentic through valley from Beckermonds by Greenfields to Birkwith, and at higher levels rather similar valleys by Cosh, Foxup Moor, and Penygent Gill. It is inevitable that from very early times these through valleys have been used as highways. Most of them are traversed by green roads.

From Ribblehead the Roman road to Bainbridge, the Cam High Road, makes its way up the spur of Cam Fell, but a branch soon breaks away to the east, near Cam Houses, continuing above the stream down to Oughtershaw. The road through Greenfields from Beckmonds is a true green road for most of its course. Starting at Beckermonds, a road goes up the north side of Greenfield Beck to Low Greenfield just before reaching which there is a branch coming back along the side of Beckermonds Scar, and swinging round the hill shoulder

to Oughtershaw, crossing through the hamlet and keeping in
a direct line up the side of the old enclosure, across Cow Close
to the boundary wall on Woldside. From here it continues in
a very straight line to the north east along the east side of
the ridge between Raydale and New Close Gill, down to Mar-
sett. This affords a few miles of magnificent moorland walk.

From Low Greenfield the Horton Road continues to High
Greenfield through some of the pastures where Arthur Young
saw the interesting experiments in land reclamation about 1774.
The farmer reclaimed " black moory land " by burning and
liming it, sowing with turnips, then laying down to grass with
ray grass, clover, hay seed, etc. Accompanying this by
sound walling, and good grazing, with some draining, over 200
acres were improved, and at the time of the visit, the land
carried 20 horses, 40 cows, 1,200 sheep, and 300 young stock
for summering, making use of the moorland pasture surround-
ing it.

Beyond High Greenfield the road comes on to the open
moor, swings south west past the abandoned house of Green
Haw, and across Birkwith Moor and is here called Langstrothdale Road. The old road swings down through Top and
Fawber to Newhouses and so on to the Cam Road from Horton, but the road that is now more commonly used continues
on the moor wall side, past Jackdaw Hole and Long Churn,
to Sell Gill Barn and so into the walled lane of Harber Scar
Lane, and down to *New Inn* at Horton.

This road was used by Fountains Abbey, who owned
Greenfield as a sheep grange and had property along this road.
After a dispute with Jervaulx Abbey it was agreed (A.D. 1224)
that Fountains should have fourteen oxgangs of land in Horton, the lodge at Birkwith and the inclosed meadow about the
lodge, and Jervaulx were to have six oxgangs and the service
of Richard the Clerk for the land around Fawber. Jervaulx
Abbey had a horse breeding farm at Horton, and used the
Greenfield road as their normal route into Wensleydale.

This road remained of some importance until well into
the eighteenth century. As a pack-horse road it formed part of
a way from Lancaster across into Yorkshire. Packs could
come by many routes to Horton, the latter stage being probably by Crummackdale and Moughton, then by Greenfield
and down Langstrothdale to Hubberholme and forward by
Cray to Aysgarth and Leyburn or by Coverdale to Middleham.

In 1693 the bridge at Hubberholme was in *great ruine and decay . . . the said bridge beinge the highe road way leading between the markett towne of Lancaster . . . and the markett towne of Newcastle-upon-Tyne and other places in the countie of Northumberland.*

This line forms a remarkably direct way if followed out on a small scale map. From Starbotton a short cut could be taken up Starbotton Cam road and by Cross Gate on to Kettlewell Cam Head and so on to the Coverdale road. None of the gradients would trouble pack-ponies, who were taken over the most mountainous country.

A somewhat similar but wilder road runs from Horton around the west flank of Penyghent to Foxup, called in part, Foxup Road. This road leaves *New Inn* at Horton, as Horton Scar Lane, running near Hull Pot and Hunt Pot. It climbs steadily round Penyghent Side, swinging steadily more to the north east to Swarth Gill Gate on the boundary wall between Ribble and Skirfare drainage, at 1,600 feet above sea level.

Round the north side of Penyghent, across Foxup Moor, it keeps nearly level along the slight shelf of the Middle Limestone then divides to drop down to Foxup or to Foxup Bridge. This is a wild and wet road, often difficult to distinguish on the moor, but it affords grand views and well repays the trouble taken to follow it out. From Foxup there is a continuation across Elder Carr Moor to Beckermonds, but this is a footpath rather than a green road.

The best known of these old roads has been modernised in surface, though the line preserves much of the original layout. This is the road from Stainforth and Settle, by Silverdale and, over the pass between Penygent and Fountains Fell, down to Halton Gill. From Stainforth the road, called Goat Lane, climbs up to Sannet Hall, crossing the two Craven Faults in its course and passing many good exposures of Silurian slates. Near Sannet Hall, Henside Lane crosses it, from Kilnsey and Malham Moor, and continues to the west as Moor Head Lane to Helwith Bridge, then by Wharfe and Austwick to the west and eventually to the Kirkby Lonsdale road and to the Lakes. This cross road comes from Fountains Abbey by Pateley Bridge and Grassington, by Bordley and on to Malham Moor, and links up in its length many of the Fountains Abbey properties. Forward from Sannet Hall the

Halton Gill road is known as Silverdale Road, as far as Dale Head and Peter Castle.

On the road side at Peter Castle there is still the base of Ulfkill Cross, an ancient boundary cross mentioned in the Fountains Cartluary and in the boundaries of Langstroth and Litton Forest. Past Rainscar House the road comes on to open moorland to the top of Penyghent Gill where it divides, a grass road going down the east side of the gill to Nether Hesleden and Litton, the modernised road on the west side going past Penyghent House and Upper Heselden to Halton Gill. The neolithic burial mound known as Giants Graves is in the first croft as the road crosses to the west side of the gill.

From Halton Gill the old pack horse road continues up Horse Head Low Pasture, then turns north east over the Horse Head Pass into the head of the Mill Beck, which runs down to Raisgill. The Mill Beck on some modern maps is called Hagg Beck.

From Raisgill the way could be followed either up dale by Deepdale and Oughtershaw into Wensleydale, or by Hubberholme and Kidstones into Bishopdale. There was until recently an old single arch pack horse bridge at Deepdale not unlike the one still standing at Yockenthwaite, and we have already mentioned the importance of the bridge at Hubberholme. These pack-horse ways were in use up to about a century ago and, even in living memory, pack-horses carried coal to Kettlewell Smelt Mill from Gargrave, and lead across the moors from many of the smaller mills to Grassington. Roofing slates for housing were a frequent commodity in the upper parts of Wharfedale, being brought out of Coverdale for use in the area below Kettlewell, and from around Beckermonds and Cosh for the upper parts of Wharfedale and Littondale.

Coal was carried from many of the small hill-top collieries, such as that on Fountains Fell, and there are many old pack ways winding down the steeper fell sides now appearing as multiple winding trenches, old ways being worn deep and becoming stream beds in wet weather, and new ones being made alongside, time after time. Tracks of this character can be seen clearly along Rilstone Fell Edge, from the small outcrop coal workings in the Millstone Grit, coming down to the various villages.

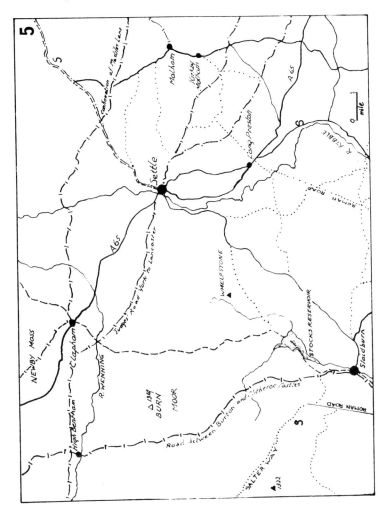

From the head of Airedale there are many ways across
Malham Moors, which probably originated as tracks and were
made into good horse or bridle gates by the tenants of the
many Fountains Abbey farms. As most of Littondale and all
Malham Moors belonged to this abbey, there was great coming and going across the fells, much moving of flocks of sheep,
getting of peat and stone, and some hunting. One of the
tracks that linked up many of their properties has been made
into a good road and is now very well known, that from Malham
by Tarn House and over Darnbrook to Arncliffe. Less used
and still remaining as green roads or trackways are the two
from Street Gate to the east of the Tarn, one by Middle House
and Flask to Arncliffe, and the other by High Mark to Hawkes-
wick Cote. Both these ways are well made, and remain for
most of their length as a clear, wide green track almost a road.

The dominant road of Malham Moor is, of course, Mastiles
Lane running from Kilnsey, with a branch from Threshfield
and Skyrethorns over the Bordley Moor, Malham Moor and
forward to Helwith Bridge and so westward. This was a main
road for the monastic traffic and is marked by wayside crosses
(now the bases only) at several points along its length. (For
more details see the Dalesman book on *Malhamdale*). Nearly
parallel to this, but of less importance, is the bridle way from
Threshfield and Linton, by Boss Moor, the head of the Winterburn valley by Lainger House, and so to Gordale and Malham. From Malham it continues by Hoober Edge as a footpath, or up the Ewe Moor as a broad pack-horse way, over
Grizedale and to Stockdale, and so to Settle. This gives a
very direct way by Malham and Grassington, from Settle to
Pateley Bridge and Ripon.

The portion of this road beyond Grassington was converted into a Turnpike road by an act of 1758: *An Act for
repairing and widening the Road leading from Wetherby
through Spofforth, Knaresborough, Ripley, Scoroe, Pateley
Bridge, Greenhaugh Hill and Hebden to Grassington in said
county of York.* The road was surveyed and made, and milestones set up along it. Many of the milestones remain today,
small triangular section pillars with P and B and the miles on
two faces. The accounts of the Trustees include the item
" Paid William Tomlin for Cuttin and Dressing, Lettering
and Setting, etc. Milestones from Pateley Bridge to Grassington, £3 : 9 : 10d." With ten stones to get and set, this was

not by any means a generous rate of payment. The only Toll Bar between Grassington and Pateley was on Greenhow Hill, the first house on the left as the Hill is approached from the Dry Gill side.

The main road up Wharfedale hardly comes within the title of green roads, but there are fragments of the old road that are now grass grown, and are worth passing mention. An old map of Yorkshire, that by Badeslade, 1741, shows one of the principal north roads coming from Halifax by Keighley and Skipton, then into Coverdale via Wharfedale, and so forward to Middleham and Richmond. This was for some time a coach road that was well used. In Wharfedale, past Threshfield, the old line diverges from the present road opposite Netherside Hall, and is followed as a green road along the west side of the plantation, over the hill summit past a Bronze Age tumulus, as usual situated on a wonderful view point. Down the wall side, the road is joined by the straight portion of modern road, at the foot of Kirk Bank, and the two are on the line almost to the roadside quarry.

The old road goes forward in a direct line to the river and is seen as a hollow way with large boulders here and there set along the edge of it. For a quarter of a mile it runs on the river bank, past Mill Scar Lash then makes across Broad Ing to be joined again by the new road just beyond Chapel House. It is about fifty years since the new road was cut.

From Conistone a green road climbs the fells to the north of the village, turning off the Kettlewell road just beyond the Church. It is called Scot Gate Lane in its early part, then when it passes the Moor Gate on to Conistone Moor, it becomes Bycliffe Road. It divides and one section goes north to Conistone Moor at Cappleside Gate, turns along the moor wall side and at the next gate joins Silver Rake, the green track from the Mossdale mines to Kettlewell. The east branch goes over rough country into Mossdale, past the old mines just beyond the old shooting box. From Mossdale the road continues into Nidderdale as the Sand Gate.

From this branch of the road, at the summit of Kelber barely two miles from Conistone, a green road strikes southeast on the ridge between Gill House and Barrus, and after a short walled stretch and another longer stretch over open moor, becomes Limekiln Lane, a grass lane leading directly to Yarnbury above Grassington. This, with the green road that goes forward from Yarnbury on to Grassington Moor, is mainly a peat and mine access road, leading only from the villages to the moors, and not crossing into the next valley.

Limekiln Lane, from Conistone Moor to Yarnbury, can be continued by going through the gate opposite Yarnbury House, past the first of the old mines, keeping right at the fork, and down into Hebden Gill and to Hebden. Again, the road that keeps on to the moor, the left branch of the fork, the Dukes New Road, is only an access road to the mines and does not continue past them.

In all parts of the Dales these green roads lead out of the villages on to the moor tops, then die out, only very rarely being continued over the fell to the next dale. An exception is the Top Mere Road at Kettlewell, the well known, widely seen green road that climbs steeply out of Kettlewell up the shoulder of Kettlewell Cam. Near Cross Gate this joins the road from Starbotton at Hunter Stone, swings round the contours at the head of Cam Gill and joins the Park Rash road into Coverdale. An old track goes forward from Cross Gate across Starbotton Peat Ground and Tor Mere Top, then along the boundary wall between Starbotton Moor and the head of Waldendale, on the Walden side of the wall. From the corner of the first cross wall on that side, the track makes down rapidly to the head of the Walden Beck and so down to the road down the dale to Walden and West Burton. This, which is shown as a good track on old maps, becomes a footpath on the 1865 surveys and drops out of later editions, being now hardly traceable past Tor Mere Top.

Similar green tracks which are now hardly more than footpaths but which in the past have been used by pack-ponies, are those from Kettlewell to Arncliffe by the Slit, from Litton to Hubberholme (used by the parson while Hubberholme was a chapel at ease from Arncliffe Church) and from Arncliffe to Starbotton.

21   An old packhorse track from the Grassington Moor Mines, which was abandoned in 1790 when Moor Road was made.

22   A peat road on Grassington Moor with stacks of peat drying alongside.

23 Porridge Stoop, dated 1730 at the crossing of two very old roads from Skipton to Colne and Keighley to Clitheroe above Lothersdale. This was formerly the site of a market for oatmeal and salt, both brought by packhorse trains. *(A. Butterfield)*

24 The clapper bridge, ford and packhorse bridge at Linton about 1890. The footbridge was removed to the other end of the village in 1892 when a bridge replaced the ford and stepping stones brought here.

25   A thirteenth-century cross on
an old road on the boundary of
Langstrothdale Chase in Upper
Wharfedale.

26   A packhorse bridge on the
old track from Ilkley to Ripon at
Thornwaite, near Darley in
Nidderdale. *(B. Unne)*

27   A deep-sunk packhorse way from Skipton to Halifax at High Jackfields, Sutton.
This is part of a lime road which goes by Slippery Ford and Limers' Road. *(A. Butterfield)*

28   Packhorse with barrels for lime at a lime kiln from Payne's *Microcosm,* 1803.

6 Upper Nidd and Colsterdale

THE piece of country which is approximately bounded by the river Cover, the Ure from Middleham to Ripon, the road from Ripon to Pateley Bridge, and the river Nidd above Pateley, offers some good examples of ancient roads, now mainly represented by bridle roads and footpaths, with a few better marked green roads and second or third class unfenced roads.

Much of this area, in fact all except the actual valley slope of Coverdale and the parish of Masham, lies within the ancient Honour of Kirkby Malzeard and the Forest or Chase of Nidderdale, and its ancient roads are dominated by this fact. This area passed soon after the Norman Conquest to the Mowbrays, who had a castle at Kirkby Malzeard, from which the area was ruled. Although it is now only a moderate sized village, Kirkby Malzeard was then, through many centuries, a centre of administration, the place where the lord's courts were held, where the principal market was settled, and where the mother church for the area was built.

When the Mowbrays granted much of Nidderdale to the monks of Fountains Abbey, and when Jervaulx and Coverham Abbeys were also well established, minor centres of importance grew up around them and new roads came into use between them and their estates. The fact remains however, that upper Nidderdale and the country between it and the Ure were linked closely with Kirkby Malzeard and with Masham through most of their history, and it was not until late in the eighteenth century when the Pateley Bridge to Ripon Turnpike road was made, that Nidderdale turned more to Ripon as its natural market and outlet.

Kirkby Malzeard was granted a chartered market in 1307, to be held every Monday, with a fair on the eve, the day, and the morrow of the feast of the Nativity of St. Mary, and the eve, the day and the morrow of St. Nicholas. Byland Abbey had grants of land in upper Nidderdale, and along with Fountains and other tenants of the Honour, attended at Kirkby Malzeard market for much of their trade. In 1184 an agreement was made between Fountains and Byland Abbeys, that

63

in return for certain concessions, Byland was to have 35 acres of arable land in Kirkby Malzeard for the raising of provender for their pack-horses. This would be necessary, as Kirkby would be a resting place on their long journey from the Abbey to their granges in Nidderdale, and also there would be large numbers of pack-horses coming in to the market and fairs at all times. In other agreements between these two monasteries, there are fragments of information about roads at a very early date.

It is clear that there must have been from the twelfth century a good deal of traffic through Kirkby Malzeard from Byland, and forward into various parts of upper Nidderdale. Add to this that most of the tenacies in the Honour carried the obligation of attending the Courts of the Honour at Kirkby, held every three weeks, and that the ecclesiastical centre was also there, and it is obvious that it must have been true for a long period that "all roads (from upper Nidderdale) lead to Kirkby Malzeard."

As Fountains Abbey grew in importance and developed its estates in the mid valley of the Nidd and in the upper Wharfedale and Malham districts, a road further to the south came into importance, centred on Fountains Abbey. The Grassington to Pateley Bridge road has been mentioned in an earlier chapter, and much Fountains traffic passed along this, continuing from Pateley over Sawley Moor, and through Sawley to Fountains. From lower in the dale, the bridge at Dacre was of importance, and an old road went from that crossing of the river by Brimham Lodge (where Fountains had a grange) and by Sawley Hall to the Abbey. These roads are now modernised and can be omitted from this account.

The agreement between Fountains and Byland Abbeys, by which in 1184 Byland received the land for raising pack-horse provender in Kirkby Malzeard, continues—

Bylands is also to have full right of a road for cattle and waggons and horse loads through Wacldesheng towards Sixfoot as far as the Nid, and another road which Fountains has through the moor and wood towards Burtheit as far as the water. But Byland is not to feed horses or cattle, nor unyoke with their wagons in the pasture or herbage of Fountains except with their consent. Byland may have a bridge across the Nid between Rasegile and Burtheit.

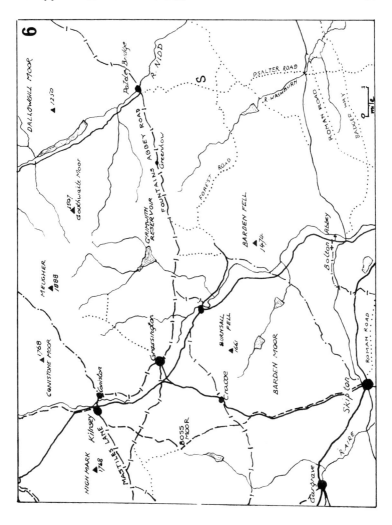

In 1198 this grant of a road is confirmed with the addition of

the other road going from Malseard to Ramegile and so to Mildesmore, and where without great cost and trouble they are not able to have their own road they may go by Lofthusum until they come to their own road again. They shall likewise have a road from Ramesgill to Hirefeld, by Sandholme, where they can have it without great inconvenience to the monks of Fountains.

This last mentioned road from Ramsgill is on the west side of the Nidd, and goes by the present farm of Highfield and Heathfield, into Ashford Gill, where Byland may have worked lead mines in the early thirteenth century. The lead and materials going to and from these and other mines would be carried by this road to Ramsgill where they had their bridge over the river to Bouthwaite (Burtheit) which was a grange of Fountains Abbey.

From here the road can now be followed up the steep ridge of ground to Intake Gate and on to Covill House Moor (Covilhouse was also a grange of Fountains Abbey) which it crosses to the north-east, passing just south of Harry Cross Stoop at about 1,260 feet OD. It then descends gently across North Gill Beck at Stope Bridge, turns east along Dallowgill Moor side past Dalton Lodge, and then takes a direct line, slightly north of east across Sweeton Moor and to Kirkby Malzeard.

Near Dalton Lodge, in the head of Dallowgill, there are the remains of an old road, now called Potter Lane, which crosses the beck and rises on to the flank of Kettlesing Hill, and then takes across Sigsworth Moor and down to Gouthwaite. Grainge, writing in 1863, says that an ancient road was found on Sigsworth Moor, apparently leading to Potter Lane, and that the road was upwards of four feet wide, paved with stones, which for some length were taken up and used in the construction of fence walls, when the enclosure was being carried out. This piece of road was most likely that part mentioned in the grant as going by Wacaldeshing—i.e. Kettlesing, toward Sixford (Sigsworth), and the paving would be the usual row of large flagstones so often placed where the road was mounting a soft bank or crossing bad ground, for the benefit of the pack-ponies.

From Dalton Lodge to the east right to Kirkby Malzeard this is now a modernised secondary road. At Intake Gate there is a branch track along the wall side going north on to Middlesmoor road, joining it where the branch to Masham leaves it, so that this would form a fairly direct road to Masham from Ramsgill. A walled lane called Sypeland, which branches off to the west, half a mile beyond Intake Gate, is a lane and access way made at the Enclosures, and is not so very old.

The next road is the one from Middlesmoor, crossing the Nidd at Lofthouse, then climbing by the hill with the curious name Blue Burnings, to the Moor Gate. Beyond this point the road has the old name Trapping Hill, climbing on to Lofthouse Level. At the head of Backstone Gill this road continues forward north-east into the head of Agill on its way to Jervaulx Abbey and Middleham, but the Kirkby Malzeard and Masham road turns abruptly east south of Ouster Bank. Just east of Black Gutter Bridge it passes an old boundary stone, Pilsden Cross (mentioned in 1259) with the curious natural rocks, Jenny Twigg and her daughter Tib, on the moor, a third of a mile to the south east.

On Combs Fell, the road from Intake Gate joins it, and here the Middlesmoor track bifurcates, the Kirkby Malzeard branch keeping nearly due east across Summer Edge and by Maiden Crags into the head of Black Dike Gutter. Here, once more, the Black Dike is a boundary and the association of *black* place names with ancient boundaries, is again demonstrated.

Across Kirkby Malzeard moor the track is in very poor condition, but at Stock Beck House comes into a macadamised road leading direct to Kirkby Malzeard. Returning to the branch for Masham, this goes by Writhen Stone, Arnagill Moor, Masham Moor, and into the head of Cat Gill, and so to Ilton, where it becomes a modern road by Warthermarske to Masham. This is a road of magnificent views of great variety; views are got over the greater part of the upper Nidd valley, across the wide rolling moorlands for several miles of the summit ridge, and finally the prettiest and more wooded views of the Leighton valley with the reservoirs in the valley bottom to remind one of the Lake District.

There is a branch road from the Masham track, leaving

it at Low Langwith and crossing Grewelthorpe Moor into the
valley of the Wreaks Beck.   Where the road climbs the north
bank of this valley as a narrow winding lane, there is the significant place name Foulgate Nook, and one can imagine this
being a most appropriate name when the road down the soft
shaly bank was slippery with deep mud and the ford at the
bottom none too clear.   Bramley Grange, belonging to Fountains, is immediately to the north-east of Foulgate Nook and
an old cross road goes through it and forward to Ilton Grange,
on the Masham road.

The tracks which focus on Kirkby Malzeard have seen
very varied passengers.   The commonest sight would be the
long trains of pack-horses carrying wool and grain to the
abbeys, and food back to the granges.   There was a small
trade in charcoal, and many packs of lead, for Kirkby Melzeard
for a time was one of the most important lead markets in
West Yorkshire.   Salt was carried into the dale, iron brought
from the forges in Nidderdale to the market and to the various
granges in the Vale of Mowbray, and as regular three-weekly
traffic, the principal tenants coming to Kirkby or to Masham
to pay their suit at the courts of the lords of the Manor or
honours.   Monks and laymen, traders and officials of all kinds
would form a common background to the life of these roads.

From Lofthouse there is a direct track across the moors to
Jervaulx, starting up Trapping Hill and keeping a very direct
line to the bridge at the head of Agill, passing the old land-
mark of Benjy Guide just on the summit.   Down the west
side of the valley it continues along the moor edge as Pott
Moor High Road dropping down Pott Bank by the Hall and
now running round the edge of the reservoir by Lealey to
Masham.   The Jervaulx road turns over the moor before the
summit of Pott Bank is reached, crosses Pott Ridge and goes
round the head of Grimes Gill down Hollin Gill to Spout
House and across Spruce Gill Beck to Gollinglith Foot.   From
Gollinglith the road climbs the north side of the valley by
Agra and up to Ellingstring Plantation, leaving Bales House
on the east.   From Angram Cote at the west end of Ellingstring, Wood Lane winds down the hill to Mellwood Cottage,
then makes a bee-line for the Abbey.

There are several tracks out of Colsterdale, as the monks
of Jervaulx had grants of coal and iron mines there in the
fourteenth century, and Geoffrey le Scrope granted to the

Abbot and Convent and all their men a free way through the whole of Mashamshire towards Colsterdale. The name Bale House is one of several names in -bale, -bole, etc., a name attached to the old iron forges and lead smelting places, the bole-hills, not as is so often claimed, a derivation from Baal and any pre-Christian worship. From Gollinglith Foot the " Coal Road " goes up the south bank of the river Burn to the several old coal pits at its head, then joins the old road from Lofthouse, Middlesmoor and New Houses, to West Scrafton.

From New Houses this green road goes by Woogill Colliery north west over the moor to the shoulder of South Haw at about 1,600 feet OD., keeping in a direct line across Steel House Moor and over the head waters of the many little tributaries to Steel House Gill. From South Haw there is a branch down into Steel House Gill passing the ruins of Steel House by which it turns sharply to the north-west and being joined by the road from Gollinglith, goes across to West Scrafton Colliery and so down Great Bank to West Scrafton.

There is a more direct bridle road out of Colsterdale to Caldbergh in Coverdale. From Colsterdale hamlet on the north side of the river Burn this road keeps around the south side of Birk Gill well up the hill side, climbing very slowly to Slip Wath, the ford at the head of Birk Gill. (This name is sometimes Slape Wath, or " slippery ford.") It crosses the moor and keeps well to the east of Ulpher Gill and by the edge of the valley gets down to Caldbergh in a pretty direct line. An old road goes forward to a ford over the river Cover near Coverham Abbey, then by Tup Gill due north over the ridge to Wensley. Much of this is now modernised.

Turning to the head of Nidderdale, there are a few old roads of interest which can still be traced. From Middlesmoor there is an almost forgotten road, though in parts it is a green road of some size, which goes up the whole length of How Stean Beck, and continues up Straight Stean Beck, the largest tributary at the head. Over Friar Hood moor it is known as the Sandy Gate, and is not difficult to follow. It passes Friar Hood Pike in Mossdale, and down by the old Fear-nought Mines becomes a broad green road from the shooting box in Mossdale. Past Mossdale Scar, where the beck disappears into the enormous cave system which is still being explored, the road crosses the old tarn bed in the head of Gill House Beck, and on Kelber divides, one branch as Bycliffe

Lane going to Conistone, the other becoming Limekiln Lane to Yarnbury and Grassington.

A better known road is the one from Lodge on the north side of Scar House reservoir, nearly due west along the hill side, rising slowly to the col between Great Whernside and Little Whernside, reaching nearly 2,000 feet OD. on the north flank of Great Whernside then making round the shoulder to the head of Park Rash, joining the Coverdale to Kettlewell road near the old Intrenchments.

From Horse House in Coverdale there is a broad green road over into Nidderdale, which was for centuries used by the Scotch drovers and pedlars, who would also use the various green roads over Flensop or Carlton Moors to West Burton and Aysgarth. From Horse House, the Cover is crossed at Arkleside Bridge, and the road goes along the south bank of the river to the ford near the foot of Arkleside Beck. Through the hamlet of Arkleside the road makes some large zig-zags up the first steep climb, then keeps up the gill side to the second stream junction, where Backstone Gill comes in. The road crosses this gill quite soon and keeps up the ridge on the east of it to Dead Man's Hill, which it crosses at 1,750 feet OD.

The traditional explanation of this name is that it was given on the discovery of the bodies of three men, preserved in the peat at that spot. It is said that they were the bodies of three Scotch pedlars who visited the dale twice a year with drapery and other goods. They had been murdered for the money they carried, and the murderers carried the bodies by sledge to this spot on the boundary of Nidderdale and Coverdale, and between the West and North Ridings, in the hope of confusing any enquiry.

The murderers were never discovered, but when the bodies were found in the course of peat cutting, the disappearance was remembered. This all took place about a hundred and eighty years ago, but the tradition is still strong. Lodge is probably named from one of the old Lodges of the forest of Nidderdale, and must have been an important place, judging by the number of tracks which radiate from it.

There are several other footpaths and tracks crossing the moors between the Nidd, Cover and Ure valleys, but an attempt has been made in this chapter to keep to those for which there is some ancient documentary evidence.

7 The Washburn Area

THE country to the west of Harrogate which lies between the rivers Wharfe and Nidd, approximately defined by the Wharfe from the junction of the Washburn north-west as far as Appletreewick, by Trollers Gill and the Grassington to Pateley Bridge road over Greenhow, by the river Nidd from Pateley to Ripley, then by the main road Ripley to Leathley and Otley, includes the whole drainage of the Washburn, and its watershed moors.

This is a widely varied piece of country with the peaks of Earl Seat and Simon Seat rising out of stark moorlands on the west which are mostly above 1,300 feet above sea level, and which include Pockstones Moor and Katty White Allotment with their wide heather-clad expanses, and the grassy, mine-riddled moors around Greenhow Hill. To the south-east these moorlands dip down to the head of the Washburn valley and to the long tongue of rough ground between the Washburn and the Bolton Bridge—Harrogate road.

Between the Washburn and the Nidd the country is lower with wide areas of grassy moorland and rough pasture, scattered farms and hamlets and a complex of small roads and by-lanes as the land becomes more and more cultivated and regulated towards the Nidd. Between the Bolton Bridge—Harrogate road and the Wharfe there is the enticing mass of Blubberhouses and Denton Moors, with the richly variegated slopes to Washburn and Wharfe.

On the modern map two roads stand out prominently, forming a cross which is fairly symmetrically superposed upon this land—the Bolton Bridge to Harrogate road, nearly west to east, making a bright red line with its " first class " colouring, and a more soberly clad road running nearly at right angles to it from Otley to Pateley Bridge, crossing it at Blubberhouses. On the east of this latter road there is the complex of small lanes and roads cutting up the country into a regular network. On the west of it lie the wild moorlands with their strong upland colouring and very few obvious tracks. The eastern part of the area calls for exploration on bicycle and by car, but the western is still the preserve of the foot passenger, and offers many ancient tracks for his exploration.

If we start with the south-western quadrant made up of Beamsley Moor, Denton Moor, and Blubberhouse Moor, there are tracks of many ages to be picked out. The best known and the one with the most precise date is, of course, the Roman Road from Ilkley to Boroughbridge, which, though it is now not continuously usable, remained for many centuries as a " highway " and still, to the east of the Washburn, provides foundation for much of the modern road.

From somewhere near the old bridge at Ilkley, the road ascends the north slope of the Wharfe valley and is probably now represented by Harding Lane and Parks Lane, running almost due north to the moor gate at the junction with Hunger Hill Road from Middleton. From this gate the road takes a definite NNE direction going to the east of Round Hill (1,341 feet OD.), the highest point of Beamsley Moor, but being lost in the soft ground south of Thatch Ling.

At the slight hollow of Gawk Hall Gill the road makes a sharp turn to an ENE direction across Sug Marsh, and soon becomes a clearly marked causeway. From the moor gate there is a footpath which keeps due north up the outside of the enclosed land then swings a little to the east, not far from the boundary wall between Denton and Middleton Moors, crossing to the east of the Roman road. From Gawk Hall Gate it cuts across Sugar Hill and joins the Roman road, where it becomes plain on the ridge beyond Sug Marsh.

At Cote Hill the road continues through the enclosed fields as a trace, while the footpath breaks away to Blubber-houses, less than a mile off. On the east of the Washburn the Roman road is for some distance incorporated in the modern road. Throughout its length from Ilkley it keeps its old name of Watling Street.

Just to the west of the Roman road as it rises up Denton Moor, there is an old trackway which crosses Round Hill to the head of Kex Gill. This path comes from the top of Parks Lane and parts from the one already described at the wall corner immediately north-west of March Gill reservoir at the crossing of Loftshaw Gill. The path goes in a direct line for the summit of Round Hill and continues due north to strike the Kex Gill road at the junction of the new and old roads.

Most of the line of this track lies near the boundary between Langbar Moor and Middleton Moor and has near it a number of names of peculiar interest. On entering on the moor at Loftshaw Gill, it rises up *Black* Hill, skirts *Black* Hill Bog, over High *Black* Hill and on to Round Hill, which on the older surveys is called *Black* Fell (Round Hill being the southern slope of this). For some reason not yet unravelled, the place name *Black* seems, in this part of the Pennines at least, to associate always with ancient boundaries, and *Black Hill* and similar named prominent points are usually at the junctions of several boundaries.

At this present Black Hill there is the boundary stone of three parishes, and one of the boundaries is that of the ancient Forest of Knaresborough. Just across Kex Gill, near the junction of this path, Pace Gate Beck is the continuation of the old forest boundary, and for two miles along the boundary is called *Black* Sike, with *Black* Bank forming the eastern side of it. At another part of this ancient boundary of the forest the *Black* name appears—near the head of Possforth Gill, the boundary runs for some distance along the side of *Black* Pasture.

A surprising number of examples could be quoted from various parts of the mid-Pennines, not only hill names but others, e.g., Black Pottes (on the river Wharfe) and Blacklowe occur in the boundary of Leathley Parish, Black Hole, Black Pot, Black Beck, etc., Black Hill again at Craven Cross on the boundary of Knaresborough Forest and scores of others.

The footpath just described does not end at Kex Gill head, but turns along the old Kex Gill road, north of the stream, for a very short way keeps NE across Nun Ings to Turnwath Bridge over the Redshaw Gill Beck and in a straight line to East Gate, as *Street* Lane, a name very suggestive of an ancient roadway. The rest of the track forward by Padside and to Dacre is a modernised road. It is probable that this is part of the old road from Skipton by Bolton Bridge, Kex Gill, East Gate, to Dacre, the bit between Kex Gill head and East Gate being now little more than footpath or green road, the rest being obscured in modernised ways.

To return to the southern edge of the Denton Moors—there is a very ancient way from Beamsley, along the moor edge to Timble and Fewston, and forward to Harrogate, that in parts preserves its old name of *Badger Gate*. *Badger* is now

an obsolete word, formerly in use in the dialects of all the
northern counties, defined by Wright in the Dialect Dictionary
as meaning a corn-dealer, a corn miller or miller's man. Originally it meant someone licensed to buy corn in one market and
sell it in another. Another usage is for a huckster or pedlar
who buys up goods or farm produce and carries them across
country to sell somewhere else, and a *Badger Gate* would be
a common name for the road habitually used by the Badger and
his train of pack ponies.

The present Badger Gate starts from Beamsley, where it
can be regarded as continuing the road from Skipton to Bolton Bridge, climbs by Goosehill and Lanshaw Bank to Beacon
Hill passing on the south flank of the Beamsley Beacon, where
it is called Badgers Gate. It passes by Wards End, just on the
edge of the enclosed land and the open moor, keeping roughly
at 900 feet above sea level for some way. It comes to a cross
roads on Longridge then continues along Longridge and Foldshaw Ridge to the head of the Hungerhill road above March
Gill Reservoir. The little diversion on to Longridge is made
to avoid the two broad glacial overflow channels of Foldshaw
Slack and Drya Dyke, both boggy and unpassable.

There is a short gap in the track from the head of Hungerhill road to the gate on to the moor at the head of the lane from
Denton to Denton Moor, a distance of about threequarters of
a mile. From this last gate the track is well marked and is
called Low Badger Gate. It then goes by Ellercar Pike along
the boundary wall of Askwith Moor and Timble to the short
lane leading to Sourby and the cross roads just east of the
farm, where it becomes a modernised road down to the head
of the reservoir and over to Fewston, with a diversion through
Timble. East of Fewston, Penny Pot Lane carries the line
to Harrogate, though there are several fragments of an older
line just south, by John of Gaunt's Castle (an old lodge of
Knaresborough Forest), and Whinhill Farm into the Oak Beck
valley.

This Badger Gate would be in great use when the Forest
of Knaresborough was disforested in the late enghteenth century and Skipton became the great corn market for east Lancashire and Craven. Corn was carried by many ways from
Knaresborough and Harrogate to Skipton (where Newmarket
Street was built for this new trade), and we can picture some
of the badgers using this way in order to include places like

Timble and Beamsley and the many farms and houses along this road. The larger traders, of course, would use the more prominent road by Blubberhouses.

Finally, for this southern portion of the area, there is a complex of old roads, mainly peat roads, coming out from Gill Beck and Timble, and splaying out across Blubberhouses Moor. Some of them have retained their names, Holdings Peat Gate, and the Gill Head Gate. The latter goes across to the main road at Kex Head and is a short cut on to the Skipton road.

Turning to the part north of the Kex Gill road, the most interesting track is that called the *Forest Road*. We are still almost entirely within the area of the old forest of Knaresborough for which regular courts were held at Knaresborough and at places within the forest, to which tenants, keepers and servants had to make frequent journeys. The Forest road starts at Appletreewick and goes by Skyreholme mill, below Percival Hall, mounting steeply up by Green Grooves on the west of Larnshaw Beck. The road forks here, and one branch goes north as Black Hill road (near the Forest boundary) to Dry Gill on the Grassington-Pateley road. The Forest road turns east across Larnshaw Beck at Eller Edge Nook, then south east over Pockstones Moor, going between the Great and Little Pockstones at a height just over 1,400 feet above sea level. South-east across the Whams it comes to the head of Harden Gill, crosses the beck and mounts Stony Bank to Red Gate, at Hey Slack.

Here the road forks. One branch goes north-east to cross the Washburn at Hoodstorth and continues as Hoodstorth Lane to Carlhow Stoop on the road from Blubberhouses to Greenhow Hill. Across the road is a short length of footpath on the old line, to Padside Head, then by Padside Hall and Thornthwaite to Darley, Birstwith, Ripley and Ripon. The southern branch goes as White Moor Road to Dukes Hill, and by Whinny Hill to Blubberhouses. The older branch of this turns through West End, along the beck side, crosses the Washburn and becomes *Scot Lane* (a significant name as we shall see), through East Gate and as a bridle road across Hanging Moor to the long road to Birstwith, passing the suggestive name of Turpin Lair. At East Gate the road already mentioned from Kex Gill Head to Dacre can be joined and followed.

The Forest road is part of one of the many long distance drove roads, by which young cattle and stock were brought from the northern markets, often from Scotland, to the great markets and fairs of the north of England. This road would be used by drovers who had come down from the north-west, possibly to Kirkby Lonsdale, then Settle, over the Malham Moors and down Wharfedale to Appletreewick and then across to the country round Ripon. The drove roads were made along quiet county byways, where feeding for the stock could be got, with accommodation pastures for frequent rests.

The Blubberhouses — Greenhow road, called in parts Sandy Gate, Redlish Road or Black Gate, and between Otley and Blubberhouses over Snowden Bank, called Psalter Gate, is an old fair road. Otley had a fair and market at a very early date (a fair was granted in 1222 and fair and market in 1248) and Pateley Bridge got a market charter in 1312. There would be considerable movement of people and merchants between these two markets, and the principal road was by Snowden Bank and Blubberhouses, up to the mining population of Greenhow Hill, with a branch through Padside direct to Pateley Bridge.

One of the very important mediaeval commodities was salt for the preservation of meat, and this was carried from Cheshire across country by " salt roads." The road through Skipton, Bolton Bridge, Blubberhouses and to Knaresborough is one such road, and the name *Saltergate Hill* occurs on it about two mile west of Harrogate. The Psalter Gate on Snowden Bank is a mistaken modernisation of the almost forgotten *Salter Gate* joining Otley and Blubberhouses.

There is a wilderness of old mine tracks, moor tracks and occupation roads between the Sandy Gate and the Nidd, which cannot be detailed here, but which are worth exploring. It is perhaps sufficient to leave the area at this point, only drawing attention to the wealth of tracks and the variety of wayfarers that must have used them. A well ordered and informed imagination can re-people them from all ages—an outline as brief as this is has enabled us to pick up traces of Roman road, drover's way, badger gate, salter's road, peat roads, and more domestic market roads and tracks.

The views to be obtained from these old tracks are often far superior to those got from the modernised valley roads, and the quiet fellowship of the moors and uplands is still a blessed retreat for the pedestrian. There is much of prehistoric and historic interest near all these tracks, as must inevitably be the case when men for many centuries have moved along these ways, and every minute of the time spent exploring and following them will be amply repaid. The best way to learn the heart of a country is still to traverse it on foot.

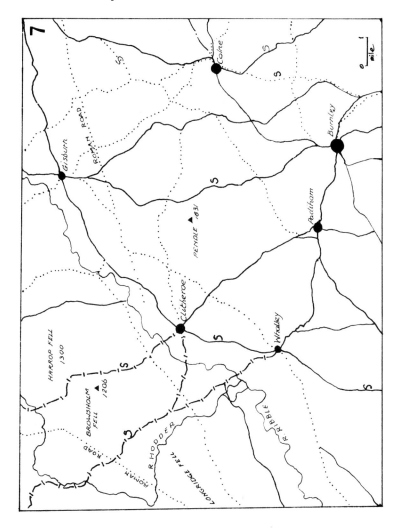

8   Baildon and Ilkley Moors

THE areas chosen so far for a description of their green roads have been remote and in the wilder parts of the Dales country. It might be interesting to vary these with an area nearer the larger towns in which green roads are abundant, if the trouble is taken to follow them out and piece together their various short bits. It has been said by some folks that Baildon was the last place made, and by others that it is the centre of Yorkshire. Whether either of these is right it is not our place to say, but in past centuries there is no doubt that Baildon has been a centre either where many green roads crossed, or as Baildoners would have it, from which many important roads radiated. Rumbalds Moor has many prehistoric remains scattered over its surface and is also crossed by many tracks, some of which may be almost of prehistoric age, but many of which are certainly very ancient.

One ancient road which crosses between Rumbalds Moor and Baildon Moor, now modernised throughout its length, deserves mention for its importance in times past as one of the great salt roads by which salt was carried from Cheshire across into this part of Yorkshire to the big markets at Otley and Wetherby. This road can be picked out near Colne where it enters Yorkshire after coming by Winewall and Wycoller Dean, with its fine bridges, up Smithy Clough and by Combe Hill Cross, to Water Sheddles Cross on the county boundaries. Part of this way by Wycoller to Combe Hill is still a green road, but from Combe Hill it is now modernised as the Colne to Keighley Road. It has to be pictured in its early condition, which lasted for many centuries, a winding green track, deep sunk as a trench up the steeper parts, and set with flagstones where the ground was soft. Fortunately portions of other roads still remain in this condition for comparison.

From Keighley the salt road climbs by Morton Banks and runs along the moor edge past *Dick Hudson's* (more correctly but less generally remembered as the *Fleece Inn*) to Intake Gate, where again popular usage has retained the name Gaping Goose after an Inn sign formerly used there. Alongside the road between *Dick Hudson's* and Gaping Goose, there

29   Drovers at Skipton, about 1840.

30   Halifax clothiers on the pack road to Leeds, on their way to the cloth fair, from
Walker's *Costume of Yorkshire,* 1814.

31 The well-paved pack road from Bingley to Ilkley at Eldwick, this part being called 'Load Saddles'.

32 A paved packhorse way on the Bingley to Ilkley road on Rumbald's Moor. On the left is a raised way for the driver.

still remain a few bits of the deep sunk old trackway. From Intake Gate the road is now a walled and modern way by Menston and Chevin End to Otley then forward to Wetherby. This road is important because along the whole of its way minor roads brought traffic up to to it for the trade in salt, which was essential throughout the middle ages and until the seventeenth centuries.

There is a branch road to join this, from Bingley to Intake Gate, much of which is still green lane and easy to follow. Rising out of Bingley there were two ways, now badly obscured by Priesthorpe and Park Side; the present road to Eldwick is pretty near on the old line, or Eldwick could be reached more directly by the road to Giltstead going by Dubb Mill and Fern Cliffe to Lane End. Here the edge of the unenclosed Gilstead Moor was reached and was crossed by the way called the Low Runagate in a nearly straight line to Eldwick Bridge. This is now almost destroyed by the quarries and enclosures, but bits of it remain here and there. By Spring Lane to Low Gate on the Bingley-Baildon boundary the track coincides with the present road, then turns up to Glovershaw Farm and Golcar Farm.

Without going through the farm yard at Golcar the road turns to the right along the field wallside to the corner of Baildon Moor. Along this part it is a well preserved paved way and is marked as such on most maps. At Golcar Gate it keeps along the moor edge for three hundred yards then enters Birch Close Lane, passes Birch Close Farm and forward to Faweather, where the group of houses and buildings mark an important road junction with Sconce Lane. Little London lies two hundred yards further along the track to the left, then after crossing the beck the road becomes Old Wood Lane, and climbs up to Intake Gate.

This road from Bingley had great importance during the monastic period when lands in Bingley, Harden and Faweather all belonged to Rievaulx Abbey and were managed from a grange at Bingley. There would be much coming and going along the road, and after the dissolution of the monasteries the old centre at Faweather remained of considerable interest and importance.

The name Little London is often given to places where traders could meet for sale of their goods, and it is likely that this and Faweather were convenient places for the pack trains with their loads of salt, iron, oil and other goods, to make a short stay while people could reach them from Baildon and the mid-Aire valley for trade. On the first road mentioned, from Morton Banks to Intake Gate, there is an old road which leaves this at Cragside Farm, comes down to Faweather and Little London, then returns to the salt road either by Old Wood Lane or by Knapley Ing.

There is another way on to the Otley Road from Bingley, by Priest Thorpe to Lower Heights farm, then by a paved road of which a good deal remains to be seen and followed to-day. Between Heights Quarry and Tewit House the track is a broad green lane, with the paving stones at one side, then near Tewit House it becomes the walled green road that is often locally called a " Roman Road," dropping down into the upper part of Eldwick Beck.

In this part the paving is very fine, and on the north side of the beck the green lane continues as a deep sunk steep trench called Load Saddles, for obvious reasons. Load Saddles comes on to the present Eldwick-*Dick Hudson* road at Low House, leaves it again to the east to go by Hoyles (or Toils) farm and across to Cragside Farm on the Otley road. This was a direct way to Otley, and carried much pack horse traffic as well as passengers on horse back. John Wesley travelled this road and stopped at Toils Farm, where his supporters of the Whitely family lived.

In Baildon the old road junction at which several tracks start lies just east of the village at Eagland's Well, at the end of Hall Cliffe. Here at least five ancient roads meet, radiating like the spokes of a wheel. The earliest of these which is documented is the road going nearly north east, starting at Ladderbanks Lane, a typical pack-horse road, dropping into Gill Beck and crossing it at the top of Tong Park Mill dam. It climbs the opposite side of the gill to Lunds Farm then turns more to the east as Straight Lane along the hill crest, joining Hawksworth Lane at Lane Side Farm, turning across the cross roads at the top of Hollings Hill and down the old lane to Guiseley and Otley.

This was a road of great importance and very busy during many centuries, as Baildon owed suit at the Archbishop's court at Otley, being one of the berewicks of the Domesday manor of Otley, while another part of Baildon was spoke of the manor of Bingley. The Archbishops secured the whole of

Baildon by 1220, and after that date the principal traffic was between that place and Otley, and the Ladderbanks Lane was the principal highway. Baildon is a very ancient market side, possibly pre-rating the Otley Market charter, and these various roads connect it with Ilkley, Bingley, Shipley, Otley, etc., for market traffic.

From Eagland's Well one of these old roads goes north as Hey*gate* Lane (which might be a Survey rendering of the older name of the High Gate) and along Moorside to Low Hill where it takes the name of Sconce *Gate*. This name—*gate* is usually found in connection with very old roads, and like the name—*street*, as in Watling Street, Stanegate, etc., goes back to the Anglo-Saxons and their dialect. From Sconce, Sconce Lane, a true green road goes to Faweather and Little London, crossing the track already described at Faweather, then swings round to Knapley Hill and crosses the Morton Banks—Intake Gate road there. After crossing Knapley Hill on the edge of the open moor, it goes north east over the moor as the Thorn *Gate* in a direct line to the head of Burley Moor Lane at Burley Wood Head. From Burley Wood Head there is a forward branch along the present moor side to Wheatley (now Ben Rhydding, a name given when the first hydros were built, as having a more genteel sound).

There is some documentary evidence of traffic between Baildon and Ilkley, and Bradford and Ilkley, and part of this road by Sconce Gate would be used by passengers between these places. It must be remembered that in olden days it was less important to have an easy graded road than to have one which called at important markets, and that the pack horse roads generally go fairly direct if a long view is taken but in small detail may be very sinuous. From Bradford, the old road came by Bolton or Idle (there are many alternative old tracks still to be followed here) either by Highfield Lane and Greenfield Lane, or a little more to the east by Thackley Town Lane, down to Buck Mill and the ford over the river Aire. This old road, still a bridle road, then climbs up to Baildon as Langley Lane, being modernised in its course north of the present Otley road.

At Baildon a diversion through the market place and up North*gate* brings the road back on to Sconce Gate and through Little London, but immediately after, where the other track swings round to Knapley Ing, this track goes forward, now only as a footpath, crosses the road and keeps up the west side of the moor wall to Horncliffe House. At Horncliffe House it bifurcates and one track goes by the old Shooting House on Grubstones, over Burley Moor just below the High Lanshaw Dam and to the head of Wheatley Rakes; the other direct Ilkley Road goes along the wall side for four hundred yards to the Laid Stoop boundary stone, crosses the wall then turns direct north and in half a mile meets the track from *Dick Hudson's* at the old guide post, and proceeds to the Lanshaw Lad (an old guide stoop) on the highest point on the moor.

Two hundred yards short of this point there is a stone circle of Bronze Age, the Twelve Apostles, almost obscured in the heather, a few yards on the east side of the track. From Lanshaw Lad the road is direct to White Wells and Ilkley. This track from *Dick Hudson's* is an old road from Bingley to Ilkley, and along it half a mile north of *Dick Hudson's* there is a finely preserved stretch of paved way.

This road from *Dick Hudson's* to Ilkley has a connection from Baildon which, starting from the general centre at Eagland's Well, goes by Hall Cliffe and West *Gate* to Tenter Croft. The short lane and footpath from Tenter Croft to Green Lane is probably the old road. Green Lane continues to Hope Hill Farm and Hope Gate, and in this section the old condition of the road is still largely preserved. At Hope Gate there is a section of the paved way still to be seen, though a portion of a longer stretch was partly destroyed during coal mining operations a century or so ago. The track is easily followed past Dobrudden Farm to Lobley Gate, then as a footpath direct to Golcar Farm. A green road continues this line through the farm yard, and to Cragside Farm on the Morton Banks— Intake Gate road, quarter of a mile west of *Dick Hudson's*.

This road from Baildon to *Dick Hudson's* can be followed forward through Morton and Morton Banks, by Holden Gate and Windgate Nick to Addingham and Bolton Abbey. There are two other old roads, now mainly marked only by footpaths, which for a long time were in use between Bingley and Ilkley and Bingley and Addingham. The first leaves Bingley by Park Road and then by Lady Lane and Walsh Lane into Height Lane on to the Otley Road a little west of Morton Stoop. From there it goes as a path cutting across Spa Flat to the wall side, the boundary between Bingley and Morton Moors, and up to the Ashlar Chair, the huge boundary stone

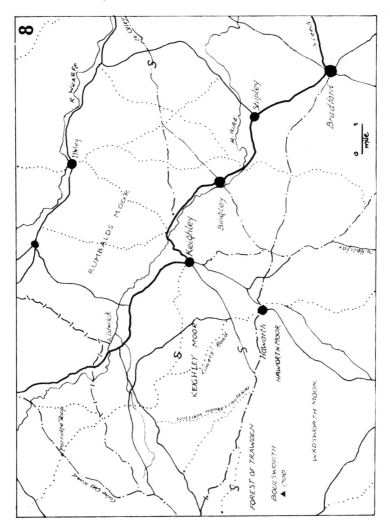

where Bingley, Morton and Ilkley Moors meet. Across White Crag Moss this joins the Dick Hudson's track in less than half a mile.

The old way from Bingley to Addingham goes by Micklethwaite Lane and Hebble Bridge or by Cross Flatts and Morton Lane to East Morton then forward to West Morton, these now being modern roads. From West Morton a portion of the old track was diverted when Upwood was built, but turning up the Ilkley Road to Bradup Bridge (with the Bradup stone circle immediately to the west of the bridge and south of the stream, and not far from the road) the old Addingham road takes out to the west at Bradup farm. This track goes very nearly due north across the moor over Bucking Hill and Shepherds Hill to Hardwick Holes, where it enters the enclosed land again. Down this valley side the way is now seen mainly as a footpath still keeping a general direction due north through two or three farms with significant names, Upper *Gate, Over Gate* Croft, *Gate* Croft. It crosses Lumb Gill just about Lumb Gill House and goes straight to the end of the road now used as the main road to Bolton Abbey, past the church.

It has been mentioned that for a time from the eleventh to the thirteenth centuries, Baildon was in part a soke of the manor of Bingley, and there would be a certain amount of direct traffic between them. At that time the Aire valley bottom would be almost impassable swamp and woodland, and a track between the two places would be sought along the hillsides and higher ground. A good deal of this can still be traced, and most of it remains as lanes and pack horse tracks.

The road due east from Bingley by Dubb Mill and Fern Cliffe would be followed to Gilstead then, before coming to Lane End, Sparable Lane turns off to the east—a typical narrow pack horse road still. This crosses Little Beck to Stubbing House and Broadstone (now sometimes called New Scarborough) at the foot of Sheriff Lane, then as the narrow track down the side of Milner Field and into the bottom of Shipley Glen, at the foot of the little reservoir.

The old name of this place is Cragg Habble, Hebble being a name always used for stepping stones and paved fords; from Crag Hebble the road has been fenced and partly straightened through the bottom of Trench Wood, then it turns up Trench Lane to Old Glen House at the corner of Bracken Hall Green (Shipley Glen). A bit of old road runs behind the first houses at the head of Prod Lane, making across towards West Lane, which formerly ended somewhere near Farfield House. This part of the old road has been broken up and lost by the building and enclosing, but from Farfield House to Baildon West Lane remains at least in part what it was.

One other old road now lost almost beyond recognition, but which will be remembered by older readers, links Gilstead with Cottingley Bridge. This was a very important bridge over the Aire, and is described in the early seventeenth century as lying on important roads; from Gilstead the road down to this river crossing was Primrose Hill, which until twenty or thirty years ago remained as a deep sunk shady pack horse road. From Cottingley Bridge the main roads went by Cottingley and Allerton, or by Shipley High Moor on to Toller Lane, the old high road from Bradford to Keighley. Ireland Bridge at Bingley was of less importance, leading only to rough tracks to Harden or Cullingworth, the old connections of these places being more with the Bradford-Keighley road than with Bingley.

9 The Lancashire-Yorkshire Border

MOST of the areas so far described have been situated in or near the wide limestone uplands or on the gritstone moors of the lower part of the Dales, but this last region stands in vivid contrast with them in most of its aspects. The great area between Halifax, Rochdale, Blackburn and Keighley is a wild upland of heathery and grassy moors, gritstone crags, deep cloughs and numerous streams, but it is traversed by busy roads which link it closely with the busiest of the industrial areas of Lancashire and Yorkshire. It is an area of old packhorse roads and paths, but most of them have been altered and modernised to meet the ever-growing demands of traffic over them and only a few fragments of old tracks remain unchanged. The roads of this area, however, have a long history and apart from their newer surface many of the roads have hardly changed their line in many centuries.

Prehistoric tracks there may be along the " edges " of the steep sided valleys overlooking the old Forest of Rossendale, perched high up on the edge of the moor, linking areas where the tiny flints of Mesolithic man or the barrows and circles of Bronze Age man are still to be found, and even though the main lines have been engineered into good roads, there are many slight tracks and depressions alongside, and mounting the fell edges which probably mark the line of the earlier footways.

The monks of Whalley Abbey, of Salley, and of other foundations, used some of the tracks when they travelled between their various granges, and small loads of iron and wool and salt found their way over these moors from grange to monastery and from village to village. The " salt ways " remained unchanged for centuries, radiating out from Cheshire and crossing into Yorkshire by many well-trod routes, the basis of modern roads. Overlying all this traffic, however, is that of the later centuries (fifteenth to eighteenth or nineteenth) when wool and woollen manufactures dominated the markets at Rochdale and Halifax, and a rapidly growing population of

textile workers had to be fed. Any account of the old roads
of this area therefore must develop itself around the varied
characters of the wool and cloth trades, and must rely more
on the pictures of past travellers than upon descriptions of
ancient tracks still to be followed as true " green roads."

The backbone of the developing cloth trade of Halifax
and Rochdale was that hardy old character, the wool "brogger."
He seems to have been somewhat indeterminate as to his exact
class and standing in the structure of the trade. He is sometimes a merchant, sometimes a chapman, sometimes almost a
pedlar, but always he seems to have travelled the Pennines
and the country further afield, buying wool in small parcels
wherever he could, either at the farm-houses or at the small
country markets, carrying it into the larger markets and there
selling it to the merchants or to the clothiers.

Sometimes he collected wool in small parcels and merely
took it to the spinner or weaver, putting it out at commission
to be prepared, and he would more correctly be classed among
the small clothiers at that stage of his development. In some
cases the wool brogger had sufficiently large-scale dealings to
employ a train of pack-horses (twenty or thirty of them at a
time) or to have several gangs travelling at once, and he must
have been a constant wayfarer back and forth over these roads,
and a regular visitor at some of the older inns.

A picture of this small clothier-cum-wool brogger or
driver, is presented in the preamble to an Act of Parliament
passed in 1555 relating to the woollen manufacture. It says :

Forasmuche as the Paryshe of Halyfaxe and other places
thereunto adjoyning, beyng planted in the grete waste and
moores, where the Fertilite of Grounde ys not apt to bryng
forthe any Corne nor good Grasse, but in rare Places, and by
exceedinge and great industrye of the inhabitantes, and the same
inhabitantes doo lyve by clothe making, for the greate parte of
them neyther gettethe Corne nor ys hable to keepe a Horse to
carry Woolles, nor yet to bye much woolle att once, but hathe
ever used onelie to repayre to the Towne of Halyfaxe, and to
some other nigh theronto, and ther to bye upon the Woolldryver,
some a stone, some twoo, and some three or foure accordinge to
their habilitiee, and to carrye the same to their houses, some iiii,
v and vi myles of upon their Headdes and Backes, and so to make
and converte the same eyther into Yarne or Clothe, and so sell
the same, and so to bye more Woolle of the Wooll-dryver, by

means of which Industrye the barreyn Gronde in these partes be
nowe muche inhabyted, and above fyve hundrethe householders
there newly increased within this fourtye years past.

Here we see how essential was the wool driver to the
small clothier, who had neither time nor means to travel more
than a few miles at most from his work, in the search for wool.
The wool driver, of course, came between the small clothier and
the merchant, acting as a middle-man, and many efforts were
made by the merchants to curtail his trade. In fact in 1552
an Act restricting the wool driver has no good word for them,
but no doubt the picture is very much overdrawn—however,
good, bad or indifferent, the driver was probably for a long
time the commonest and most important figure on the roads
we are now considering. The complaint against the drivers
starts :

Whereas by the gredye and covetous myndes as well of
suche as have the grete plentye and habundance of sheepe and
woolles as also by the corrupt practyses of dyv'se Broggars, In-
grocers, Woolgatherers and sondrie other persons . . . it mani-
festlye appeareth that the prices thereof be wonderfulye and
excedynglie enhaunsed and raysed, to the grete hurte, detri-
mente, and decay of the Realme.

Because of this the Act provided that no one but the
recognised merchants of the Staple and the manufacturer
should buy wool, and such purchases would have to be made
directly between the producer and the exporter or manufacturer. The middle-man brogger was abolished.

The protests made against this Act for the harm it did to
the small clothier of the Halifax district led to the Act of 1555,
allowing exemption in the Halifax district. Three years after
the Halifax Act the people of Rochdale petitioned that if they
were not granted exemption, then at least some thousands of
poor people would be ruined. The amount of wool they wanted
to buy was too small for the merchants to deal with, and the
clothier could not afford to travel to the upland farms to collect
it. Thus was the brogger fully established in law, and his company travelled round from farm to farm, and to the innumerable
small village and town markets to which the farmer could bring
his parcels of fleeces or wool, or to which the other clothier
could come for his modest purchase sufficient for the week's
work.

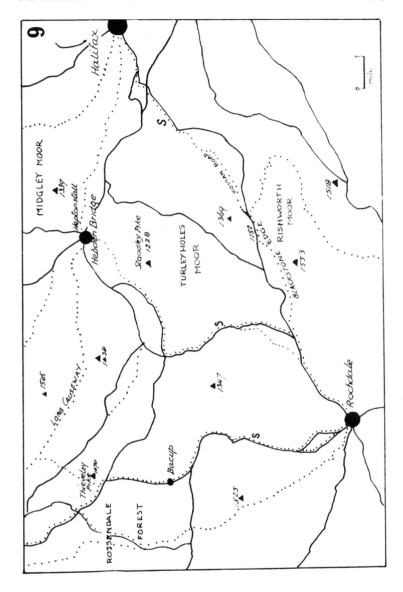

The brogger, on his never-ceasing journeys back and forth over the countryside, used and preserved many an older track over the moors. Most of them radiated from Halifax, and many of them came down to the bridge at Hebden Bridge or Sowerby Bridge as the first stage. The best known of the older roads is probably the one over Blackstone Edge from Rochdale, coming up by Littleborough, and now mainly a first-class road—not far from the line of the Roman road. For parts of its run, however, the older pack-horse road lies just to the south of it and in some parts the old pavement is well preserved.

From Rochdale to Littleborough all trace of the old road is now hidden, but after leaving Littleborough the old road branches to the south of the present Blackstone Edge road, and goes up by Windy Bank and Lydgate and then in a very direct line across the moor, passing nearly half a mile south of the Blackstone Edge Reservoir. About three miles from Littleborough, on the north-west side of Warm Withens, it drops into a deep gully and keeps on the north side of the stream as a finely-cut shelf well above the stream. It is well-paved in much of this part of its course, and has the name Dhoul's Pavement. Just after crossing Black Castle Clough it joins the newer road at New Gate End and keeps along it for a mile to Baitings Gate. Here it branches off again to the north and makes a direct way for Sowerby Bridge and so to Halifax.

This is the line so admirably described by Defoe about 1727. He says that the traffic of merchants and others had so increased of late that a new Cross Post had been lately established from Plymouth by Bristol and the Midlands to Liverpool, then eastward by Manchester, Rochdale, Halifax and to Hull. He mentions a very great market at Rochdale for Kersies and " Half-thick " cloth. Defoe and his company mounted the hills from Rochdale although snow had fallen overnight, but by the time they were at the top of Blackstone Edge they were almost in panic because of the snowstorm into which they had run. They had decided to turn back when *one of our Men called out to us, and said he was upon the Top of the Hill, and could see over into Yorkshire, and that there was a plain way down the other side . . . .* He had no great opinion of the plain way, but says *there was indeed the Mark or Face of a Road on the Side of the Hill, a little turning to the left North; but it was so narrow, and so deep a hollow place on the right, whence the Water descending from the Hills made a Channel at the bottom and looked as the beginning of a River, that the depth of the Precipice and the narrowness of the Way look'd horrible to us.* They soon picked up landmarks which had been told them at Rochdale, so knew they were right. After many weary miles he sums up: *But our Case was still this; that as soon as we were at the top of every Hill we had to come down again on the other Side; and as soon as were were down we had another to mount, and that immediately . . . . From Blackstone Edge to Hallifax is eight Miles and all the Way, except from Sorby (Sowerby) to Hallifax is thus up Hill and down; so that, I suppose we mounted to the Clouds and descended to the Water level about eight times.*

A much older road than this is the one called the Long Causeway, considerably to the north-west, and running along the western edge of the Pennine moors. overlooking the valley from Burnley to Todmorden. This road, which for great lengths is paved with large flags, and is as fine a piece of pack-horse road as is to be found in the country, runs really from Burnley in a nearly south-east direction to Hebden Bridge and Halifax. In origin, however, it is most probably connected with Whalley Abbey, as it links that place with a great many of the manors and properties they possessed along the Lancashire and Yorkshire border. From Whalley the road is direct by Padiham to Burnley, then nearly east and up the moor side to Hollins, turning then a little more south to Mere Clough. It is here that the real Long Causeway begins, and mounts from about 1,000 ft. OD. to over 1,200 ft. OD.

Its length is marked by a number of wayside crosses, many now destroyed, but their number and character strongly support the monastic origin of the road. As a piece of engineering of early date also the causeway is too large a job for any but a wealthy community such as a monastery to have undertaken. *Stump Cross* is passed first, then at less than a mile from Mere Clough, comes *Robin Cross* at a place where two important side roads mount to the causeway. Mount Lane comes from Burnley via Townley Park, and the other road comes up from Holme Chapel. About a mile further is the site of *Maiden Cross,* then in succession, *Duke's Cross* and *Stiperden Cross.*

A late diversion of the road breaks off to the north at Stiperden Cross and goes round the valley head by Stiperden Bar and back to the Causeway at the head, a second Mount Lane coming up from Cornholme. *Stone Cross* stands on this road side three hundred yards south of the Causeway. At Hawks

Stone the road turns east and crosses Bride Stones Moor, by
Blackshaw Head, then by Mytholm, Wadsworth and Midgley to
Halifax. This part across the moors probably owes more to the
broggers than to the monks.

The moors are full of fragments of other roads, and a few
can be traced in their entirety. There is a very old route from
Burnley, starting out with the Long Causeway as far as Hollins,
then turning across to Worsthorne over Hameldon and by Gorple
into the head of the Hebden valley near Widdop Reservoir.
Another track continues the road up the Hebden valley by *Widdop Cross* and Thursden across to Colne and with a branch
to Trawden. This is one of the old ways across Trawden Forest
and would be used by tenants going to the Forest courts held
sometimes at Trawden and sometimes at Colne.

From Burnley a nearly direct old road goes by Rowley
Bridge and Extwistle Hall to Thursden and then up to the reservoir head at Shuttleworth Pasture. Here it turns across the moor
just under the steep breast of Boulsworth Hill running in a due
nor-east line to meet the Colne to Keighley road at *Combe Hill
Cross,* just west of the Ponden Reservoir. This road traverses
the edge of the Forest of Trawden. From Colne there is a road
by Caister Cliff and Deerstone Moor to Widdop Cross, then
across Heptonstall Moor by Clegg Foot and *Reaps Cross* to
Heptonstall and so to Halifax.

Practically all these roads are marked by wayside crosses,
and this is some evidence that they were in use in monastic
times, probably being used mainly by tenants going to pay suit
and service at the manorial courts, by monastic servants visiting
the outlying properties, and by pack-horses carrying coal, lime,
iron, wool and corn to and from the monastic houses and
properties.

None of them are so clear or so unspoiled as the roads
across the limestone uplands, but perhaps the wildness of the
country they traverse and the greater difficulty of tracing them
may, for those who search them out, in some ways compensate
for their other shortcomings.

Index

Index